AIRBALLS!
Notes From The NBA's Far Side

Roland Lazenby

MASTERS PRESS

A Division of Howard W. Sams & Co.
A Bell Atlantic Company

Published by Masters Press (A Division of Howard W. Sams & Co., A Bell
   Atlantic Company)
2647 Waterfront Pkwy. E. Dr. Suite 300
Indianapolis, IN 46214

© 1996 Roland Lazenby

All rights reserved. Published 1996

Printed in the United States of America.

No part of this publication may be reproduced, stored in a retrieval system, or transmitted, in any form or by any means, electronic, mechanical, photocopying, recording, or otherwise, without the prior permission of Masters Press.

10 9 8 7 6 5 4 3 2 1   96 97 98 99 00 01

Library of Congress Cataloging-in-Publication Data

Lazenby, Roland.
       Airballs : notes from the NBA's far side / Roland Lazenby.
          p. cm.
       ISBN 1-57028-070-3
       1. National Basketball Association. 2. Basketball--United States.
   I. Title.
GV885.515.N37L385 1996   96-3616
   796.323'0973--dc20   CIP

TABLE OF CONTENTS

INTRODUCTION 1
PROLOGUE 3
A PRISONER IN MR. ROBINSON'S
NEIGHBORHOOD 5
IF YOU REMOVE ALL THE FRUITS AND FLAKES,
YOU STILL GOT THE NUTS 23
THE DREAM CONFERRED 35
BANK SHOTS 45
CHOKING A BIRD NAMED CHUCK 55
BE LIKE GRANT 65
HIGHWAY TO HELL 73
QUICK NICK TO THE RESCUE 101
HOOPS BY THE NUMBERS 111
AIRBALLS IN THE DESERT 119
CHICAGO HOPE 135
AFFAIRS OF THE HEART 149
END GAME 161
SKYWRITING AT NIGHT 183
EPILOGUE 199

Acknowledgments

I have a number of people to thank for making this project possible. First, Tom Bast at Masters Press believed in it, then turned it over to Heather Seal to edit it and guide it through the publishing process, aided by Tom Doherty, Holly Kondras and all the gang at Masters. I also want to thank David Levin and Mike Shank for research help and special thanks to Diddy Dean. Especially important were Lindy Davis at *Lindy's Sports Annuals*, Mike Emmett and Nando.net and Larry Canale at *Tuff Stuff* magazine, all of whom have offered support. Then, of course, there's my wife Karen and children Jenna, Henry and Morgan, who make the most special contributions of all.

I want to acknowledge the work of the dozens of writers who have covered the NBA, including Mitch Albom, Terry Armour, Lacy J. Banks, Jesse Barkin, Terry Boers, Clifton Brown, Kelly Carter, Mitch Chortkoff, Robert Falkoff, Bill Gleason, Bill Halls, Scott Howard-Cooper, Mike Imrem, Melissa Isaacson, John Jackson, Paul Ladewski, Bernie Lincicome, Bob Logan, Jay Mariotti, Kent McDill, Corky Meinecke, Mike Mulligan, Skip Myslenski, Glenn Rogers, Steve Rosenbloom, Eddie Sefko, Gene Seymour, Sam Smith, Ray Sons, Paul Sullivan, Mike Tulumello, Mark Vancil, Bob Verdi, and many, many others. Their work has been invaluable.

Credits:
Photos: Steve Lipofsky
Cover Design: Kelli Ternet

INTRODUCTION

An airball is the diametric opposite of a slam dunk; it's the big miss, a confidence-deflating, game-destroying gaffe; it's the secret fear every player harbors of failing badly at the biggest moments. It's also a delight for the fans, because they get to see highly paid professionals in their most embarrassing moments, when the so-called superstars reveal themselves to be very human after all. And that's the goal here — to get behind the scenes of pro basketball's staged events to look at the people who play and coach and manage "the game."

The subjects are among pro hoops' most fascinating — Charles Barkley, Michael Jordan, Dennis Rodman, David Robinson, Karl Malone, John Stockton, Jerry Sloan, Phil Jackson, Grant Hill, Hakeem Olajuwon, and others — and my effort was to find them at their best and worst, their craziest and wisest. Over the course of 18 months, from the opening of training camp in October 1994 to spring 1996, I tracked the game's best, talking right wing politics with David Robinson and learning why Barkley's teammates want to strangle him. Just as fascinating were the stars whose biological clocks are ticking, leaving them facing the fact that they may conclude their careers without ever winning a championship.

How do they perform under the weight of their own and the public's expectations? What are their fears and insecurities? Where do they find relief from past disappointments? Will they fail yet again and suffer the ignominy of long, celebrated, ultimately fruitless careers? How much do they care? Are they really dedicated, or is the money so good that they're merely putting up a sham to help the NBA perpetrate an entertainment fraud? At the moment of truth, will they shoot air balls?

Ultimately, *AIRBALLS!* is a search for what, if anything, is real about modern pro basketball. Over the past decade, the NBA's gross revenues have ballooned incredibly, making millionaires of even the most mediocre players. Even worse, some believe, the vast cash, which rescued the league from failure, has now reduced it to a heartless show, a shell game, hardly better than WWF wrestling. And many of its young superstars are considered selfish, greedy, overpaid and unworthy of "inheriting the game."

Are Barkley, Stockton, Malone, and Robinson the last of a dying breed of "real" players? Or is this dark view of the modern NBA unwarranted? Boston Celtics maestro Red Auerbach used to have a theory that the more you pay a great player, the more he tries to prove his worth. But Auerbach managed the Boston Celtics in the days before players' salaries came to rival Haiti's GNP. Does the same hold true today? Are the highly paid young stars members of a lost brat pack? Or are they just as dedicated as the "old pros?"

To help answer these questions, to escape boredom and to add to his already substantial wealth, Michael Jordan returned to basketball in March 1995. As a result, the game was immediately drowned in an outpouring of hype, making it a truly unique and noteworthy year. To chronicle it, here are my notes from the far side.

PROLOGUE

The story begins in the fall of 1994. A year earlier, Michael Jordan had abruptly retired from the NBA following the murder of his father James in North Carolina. For three straight seasons, Jordan and his Chicago Bulls had dominated the league. His departure meant that suddenly there was an opportunity for someone else to win a championship. There was a short list of players with superstar credentials hoping to lead their teams to a title. That June of 1994, Hakeem Olajuwon and the Houston Rockets defeated Patrick Ewing and the New York Knicks to claim their first championship. The championship series itself was roundly booed by fans and media alike. The physical style of the Knicks gave the seven game series a pedestrian, boorish pace that sent television ratings plummeting and left observers pining for the days when Jordan had soared to dunks while lifting the Bulls' finesse team to the top of the league.

In the wake of the 1994 NBA Finals, the league rules committee responded with drastic alterations to the game to make it more exciting. The three-point line was moved in, and there were closer guidelines for hand-checking and illegal defense. It was hoped that these changes would restore the NBA to the popular status it had enjoyed during the Jordan years.

To some degree, the new rules helped. But there was little question that the NBA still greatly missed Jordan's unique presence. He had risen to the status of a cultural icon during his decade in pro basketball. The game needed another presence as large as his. In October of 1994, as training camps opened, there was a pressure on the NBA to create yet another fantastic chapter in its book of legends. Was there anybody out there who could entertain like Jordan? Finding the answer to that would prove to be something of a burden for the league's stars.

A PRISONER IN MR. ROBINSON'S NEIGHBORHOOD

OCTOBER, 1994

It's Sunday morning in the little gym at Schreiner College in Kerrville, Texas, where the San Antonio Spurs are holding training camp. The sun filters through a skylight in the gym roof. The ball glistens. The floor glistens. David Robinson's face glistens. He is making free throw after free throw, each shot seamlessly blending into another.

Two short dribbles. Set. Swish.

And again. *Two short dribbles. Set. Swish.*

Here, in this soft October light, everything about Mr. Robinson seems the image of perfection. He wears natty black-and-white shoes that just match the black and silver of his Spurs practice sweats. And they in turn match the onyx of his 7-foot-1, 230-pound frame. Set above his narrow waist, the muscled biceps and shoulders are like caricatures. Surely they belong to somebody else. To Spiderman or the X-Men or somebody.

Two short dribbles. Set. Swish.

In fact, if you were thinking of developing a master race, this guy could be the prototype. He has a degree from the United States Naval Academy (and scored 1,320 on his college boards). He has real musical ability (keyboards and saxophone). Deep religious faith. A knack for electronics and computers. A golf score in the high 70s. Wonderful parents. A pretty young wife and a handsome two-year-old son. An evolving contract that guarantees he'll be one of the two highest paid players in the game, which this season figures to reach as much as $7 million. A scoring average to match his contract.

Did I mention the honesty? He has an incorruptible honesty.

Swish.

Even the political climate suits him. He's a self-described member of the religious right, and Bill Clinton, that scurrilous perpetrator of liberal humanist values, is falling like a turd in the polls. Yes, it seems that for David Robinson every element is a swish. Every factor, a swish.

With each succeeding free throw here, his face settles deeper into a perfect peace, giving not the slightest hint of the trouble that swirls around him and his team.

If only he could inhabit the amber of this moment forever. Sadly, he can't, and that's been the trouble for Mr. Robinson since he entered the NBA six seasons ago. He has to work in a very bad neighborhood, a crazy, frustrating place that constantly challenges his perfectly positive attitude, as if some unseen basketball grinch is behind the scenes, twisting up the knobs on all the bad things, just to see how much this guy can take.

If this grinch could take on a personality, it just might be that of Dennis Rodman, Robinson's sometimes teammate, a man given to multiple ear and nose rings, body tattoos, fits of bizarre behavior and a variety of brightly dyed hairdos. He's a Robo-cyberpunk rebounding machine, and David Robinson needs him badly, only Dennis seems too nutty to be dependable.

Yet in some ways, Dennis Rodman is the least of Robinson's problems. A host of other complicating factors litters the streets of his neighborhood. This situation would be enough to dismantle the psyches of most NBA superstars. But not David Robinson. He just keeps refusing to let that happen, just keeps reading scripture, patient as Job, all the while searching the horizon for that special ray of light that signals his redemption.

His critics — and there are critics — say that he lacks intensity, that deep down, big Dave Robinson really doesn't care. Or he doesn't care enough. He goes through the motions nicely. Puts up a good front. But way down in his gut, he really doesn't want it.

That, the critics say, is the reason he has never won a championship. Not in high school. Not in college. Not in the pros.

Robinson, of course, has heard all this many times before. He knows that the fans and the media are eager for him to follow the familiar story line. Great giant. Great talent. Tragically flawed and frustrated by his inability to win a trophy.

A PRISONER IN MR. ROBINSON'S NEIGHBORHOOD

It's a simple equation that we all love in sports. Win or lose. Because that's what games are all about.

Winners are winners, and losers are losers.

We want David Robinson to be one or the other. See him feel the pressure. See him come apart during the stress test. Or see him win. One or the other. Nothing in between. After all, isn't that what we pay him $7 mill a year for? To play his role in this drama?

He knows this, of course. Knows that the expectations are high. Not surprisingly, he's smart enough not to get caught up in them.

"That [winning a title] is probably the least of the pressures that I feel," he says, having finished his free throws and now sitting intently beside me in the courtside bleachers. "The most pressure I feel is the day-to-day living up to the tremendous ability God has given me."

The real challenge, as Robinson sees it, is to take all that he has been given and not be corrupted by it. Unlike Charles Barkley, Robinson considers himself very much a role model, a position that comes with huge responsibility. "To be able to withstand the outside pressure of the money," he says. "To be a strong example everyday."

He is, after all, the "Admiral," a nickname that harkens back to his naval academy education. He doesn't feel trivialized by it. "It's such a lofty term," he says. "Where I come from, to achieve the rank of an admiral is a long, hard-fought process. You don't just get there by being lucky. You get there by being good and consistent over a long period of time. So I've always taken it as a compliment to be called Admiral. I kind of feel like I have a responsibility to live up to that reputation."

He also acknowledges tremendous pressure to perform well every night in the NBA. And, to win that elusive championship while the opportunity presents itself. That pressure has grown with each season, and now that he has turned 29, it rises yet another notch on the scale.

"You never know what's going to happen next year," he says. "So this is it for us right now. That's how I approach it. When I talk to the media, when I talk to the players, I have that in the back of my mind. This could be our last year. So we have to do it all now."

SPUR OF THE MOMENT

If you wanted to be polite, you could call it bad luck, but really it's just a profound case of lousy management.

Since Robinson came to the Spurs six seasons ago, the team has been a classic revolving door. He has played for five head coaches in six years. It seems that almost every season the lineup around him is torn apart and talented gems like point guard Rod Strickland are shipped off to make other franchises better.

Not surprisingly, this instability has cost the Spurs in the postseason. Never in Robinson's first five campaigns have they managed to win a seven-game playoff series, and three times they've been ousted in the first round. This, despite averaging better than 52 wins and taking two divisional titles.

For 1995, the entire deck in San Antonio has been reshuffled yet again, including a new owner (Robert McDermott), new general manager (Gregg Popovich) and coach (Bob Hill). As their first order of business, they deleted seven players from last year's roster and replaced them with yet another seven new faces.

The result is an interesting mix. Robinson's teammates now include the wild and crazy Rodman; the grumpy, old, mumbling Moses Malone; and brash and outlandish Chuck "The Rifleman" Person. Two others — point guard Avery Johnson and forward Terry Cummings (an ordained minister) — are as deeply religious as Robinson himself. The center laughs when asked about the disparate personalities on the roster. "Strong personalities can make or break you," he says. "You gotta have that, though. It's a must ingredient just because when the times get tough, guys have got to be able to dig down. They've got to have their own unique personalities. When you've got too many followers, too many wishy-washy guys, then it's hard to really have some character. But these kind of guys can stand on their own and carry a team during the tough times, the times when you're fragmented."

Those times have been far too frequent over the past seasons. Like any family constantly torn by division, this is not a close-knit group. They have their allegiances, but as Robinson says, the departures have been frequent, which means that every loyalty comes with a caveat, with reservation. The Spurs are something like a foster home, where the kids have been ripped off by the system so much, they've become hardened. It's only natural that people in such a situation focus on preserving the self. This, of course, is true of many pro sports franchises. But not the best ones. The best ones find a way around these cynical circumstances. And that's why Robinson had so much hope for Lucas. Because the enthusiastic coach had made the place seem like a home, even if that home was the basketball version of "Boys Town."

Now, Lucas, too, is a "departure."

And the process of building that special atmosphere must be restarted. Fortunately, Robinson remains untouched by cynicism. He has kept the faith through each setback. Now he must employ it once again to rebuild this team.

The latest changes have been made, management says, to get "a fresh start." Yet Robinson has seen nothing but "fresh starts" in his tenure here. It's just a euphemism for "departure." Words like "continuity" and "patience" and "consistency" would be more welcome.

Nevertheless, "fresh start" it is, and to effect that, Spurs management has decided to bring the team here to Kerrville, a little city that hunkers down along the Guadalupe River as it bends its way through the Texas Hill Country. The main industry here — outside of housing for rich retired people — is "exotic" game hunting, which is a neat disposal system for worn-out zoo animals that a local rancher dreamed up several years ago. Overnight the idea boomed, making the Kerrville area home to a number of "preserves" and shooting schools. (Want to kill a zebra without having to waste all that time going to Africa? Come to Kerrville. The animal may be old and require a bit of prodding to get it moving, but, hey, it's a zebra, something you can mount on the wall back in the office.)

Most of the Spurs aren't too interested in hunting, although their headquarters is the local Holiday Inn, a converted hunting lodge resplendent in the number of severed and stuffed "exotic" game heads mounted on the walls. Likewise the furniture in the lobby is all rustic wood and animal skins. There's even a stuffed, erect grizzly, frozen in midgrowl for the visitors. It's a laid-back little setting, a perfect place to hide away your basketball team in hopes that it will get an unencumbered start to the season. Sadly, the season is only hours old and already encumbered. On Friday, Rodman missed a team meeting, then failed to make the team bus from San Antonio to Kerrville, leaving his teammates and Spurs management fuming and the local media scurrying to find out just what the mercurial forward was doing.

At 33, Rodman presents quite an enigma. Is he a rebel fighting off the corporate devils who would suck the life and enthusiasm out of pro basketball? Or has Rodman merely become a master showman, able to manipulate substantial media coverage with his antics? No one, not even Rodman himself, seems to know.

From a much-publicized fling with Madonna last spring, he has bounded to a special marketing level that has prompted Nike, whose athletic shoes he endorses, to produce a holiday television advertisement in which Rodman roughs up and intimidates Santa Claus. This, of course, stands in substantial contrast to Robinson's own Nike commercial from a few seasons earlier that espoused education and family values and warned drug dealers and other slimeballs not to venture into "Mr. Robinson's Neighborhood."

"Mr. Robinson doesn't like garbage in his neighborhood," Robinson declared with a menacing glare.

The menace now, though, is Dennis. His missing the team bus is bringing just the kind of spotlight that the Spurs' new management had hoped to avoid. In fact, the team had moved its training camp to Kerrville at the last minute just to get away from San Antonio and any controversy. The management even hired off-duty local cops as armed guards to make sure that reporters don't snoop too close to practice and get an idea of any new secret plays that coach Bob Hill is installing.

"The press doesn't attend meetings at General Motors or Xerox, and this is really the same thing," explains Hill, who in three seasons as the coach of the Indiana Pacers directed his teams to the playoffs, where they, like the Spurs, failed to win a seven-game series. "There are times," he adds, "when a team has to be sequestered to grow."

Or maybe just to survive another Rodman media blitz.

Whatever the reason, the Spurs are hiding out here in the hills, and reporters are allowed in the gym only at the end of the practice, when the players are shooting free throws, which is about all I've seen of Robinson. After practice, he's been pleasant enough about coming over to sit in the bleachers and answer my questions. But each interview session lasts only about 15 minutes, which means that I'm spending more days in Kerrville than planned. Soon I begin thinking that if there's a prisoner in Mr. Robinson's neighborhood, maybe it's me.

Waiting here has been a bit unnerving because it reminds me of the small town in Virginia's Blue Ridge Mountains where I grew up. Back in the 60s, we'd ride around town, traveling the same roads over and over again, seeking some relief from the boredom, venturing out past the town limits a ways before turning around and doing the whole thing all over again. Here, in Kerrville, it's much the same. I've seen the local Wal-Mart from every possible angle as I cruise around in my rental car between sessions of training camp. All I have to look forward to are the interviews with Robinson after hours of riding around or standing outside the gym with the armed security guards.

I'm almost desperate enough to go shoot some tired-ass old zebra.

A PRISONER IN MR. ROBINSON'S NEIGHBORHOOD

Today, as Robinson settles down onto the bleachers beside me, I remark that, regardless of its merits, change itself is a difficult thing.

"Yeah," he agrees.

Has each change presented a new leadership challenge for you? I ask.

"I just try to stay real positive," he says. "I think that the main thing you can give your guys is the confidence. You gotta let them know that you believe in them, that you know you can win. When you take that away, I don't think you have a chance. I just try to keep their spirits up and keep their focus off the 'minor inconveniences.'"

He laughs when he says "minor inconveniences," and this gives me pause. Has a tinge of cynicism crept into his attitude?

Many observers thought coach John Lucas' departure after the 1994 season would be the blow that pushed Robinson to the brink of despair. The center and effervescent coach had grown very close during Lucas' two seasons in San Antonio.

"It was tough at first when I heard Luke was gone," Robinson admits. "I was a big fan of his, and I thought that as he grew as a coach we were gonna be a much better team. I was disappointed, but you don't really have time in this league to sulk over departures. People depart every day. I've faced that for the last five years, so I don't really worry about it. I felt like no matter who they brought in here, my job was gonna be difficult, and I was gonna have to come out and get it done."

That sounds good, but the 1994-95 season has yet to begin and already his path is obstructed by more strange challenges, the strangest of which is Rodman, who shrugs off the complaints of the Spurs' new general manager, Gregg Popovich. Over the next few days Popovich will throw up his hands and finally ask Rodman, "How am I supposed to deal with you?"

"You'll have to figure that out for yourself," Rodman will shoot back.

Figure Popovich must, because the 33-year-old Rodman presents the Spurs' real hope for winning. His arrival before the 1993-94 season brought tremendous help for Robinson. Rodman was the type of rebounder and defender at power forward that a great center must have to be successful. He had proven that during his first seven seasons in the NBA while helping the Detroit Pistons win two championships. The Spurs had traded for him before the 1993-94 season in hopes that he could play the same role in San Antonio. The payoff was immediate. With Rodman playing beside him and pulling down a league-leading 17.3 rebounds per game, Robinson was turned free to terrorize opponents.

He led the league in scoring in 1993-94 with a 29.8 average and rang up 10.1 rebounds and 3.31 blocks per game. Playing as a point-center in the Spurs' attack, he zipped 4.8 assists per game to his teammates, one of the greatest passing displays ever by an NBA center (he also led the league in triple-doubles with five).

"Point-center" meant that Robinson actually ran the Spurs' half-court offense like a point guard, a task beyond the talents of most NBA centers. "It was great," he says. "You're running the offense. You have a lot of say-so in what's happening. The guys who are hot, you can get the ball to them. It was fun. I was distributing the ball a lot. I made guys cut; I got to see the floor and then create some things for myself when I wanted. I don't think that teams could stop it as long as I got the ball where I wanted to get it."

As a young player in Detroit, Rodman had earned a reputation for boundless energy and enthusiasm and a willingness to run through walls if that's what Pistons coach Chuck Daly wanted. Rodman himself said many times that he saw Daly as a father figure. When they won their championships together in 1989 and '90, Rodman was overjoyed. But that exhilaration soon turned to distrust and disappointment after a clash with Pistons management forced Daly to leave the organization in 1992. Plunged into depression, Rodman threatened suicide, then became rebellious and antagonistic. He hated Pistons management, and through a series of confrontations and displays of bizarre behavior in games, he forced his trade to the Spurs.

First he missed all of Pistons training camp in October 1992, saying that his divorce and Daly's departure had left him with little desire to play. Then in November of '92, Rodman refused to go on a road trip, so the Pistons suspended him for three games. A few months later in February of '93, he again drew attention with press reports about an incident in which he had supposedly threatened to harm himself and was later found sleeping in his truck in a parking lot at the Palace of Auburn Hills. That March, he was suspended another game for missing practice.

Unfortunately, he brought his anger with him to San Antonio. Throughout the 1993-94 season, Rodman's oncourt outbursts played a discordant note to Robinson's Mr. Clean approach, resulting in fouls, fines and suspensions for the power forward. The first major incident with the Spurs came in December 1993 when he was suspended a game and fined $7,500 for head-butting Chicago Bull Stacey King. Three weeks later, in January of '94, he was fined $10,000 for failing to leave the court and verbally abusing the referees. March 1994 brought another one-game suspension and a $5,000 fine for head-butting Utah's John Stockton. Lucas attempted to accommodate Rodman's individuality, allowing him to wear zebra-striped sweats to practice, or to avoid practice altogether, or to miss the team bus to the arena for games. But that policy was deemed a failure when Rodman acted up in the first round of the playoffs against the Utah Jazz and was suspended for a critical game. The Spurs lost, terminating their playoff drive and Lucas' tenure in Texas.

In the aftermath it could have been a convenient out for Robinson, to blame the Spurs' woes on Rodman. But the center said anyone who did that "was just looking for an excuse." Robinson said the Spurs lost because they — particularly himself — didn't play well.

Mostly, the playoff loss revealed that the team needed more than the point center offense, because it left them trying to pound the ball into the basket on every possession. "It just makes too many baskets too tough," Robinson says. "I enjoyed playing that way last year. Obviously it was a great showcase for my abilities. But I'm interested in winning games."

To make the change and instill discipline, the Spurs hired Hill and installed a running game, of which Rodman's rebounding and ability to run the floor are supposed to be major factors. But, already Rodman shows signs that he's just not going to cooperate, that he's intent on playing a bone-headed devil to go along with Robinson's patient angel.

Even now, with Rodman having started the year all wrong, Robinson defends him. "Don't be fooled," he says. "Dennis is a bright guy. When it comes to basketball, he understands the game, understands what needs to get done. He studies a lot of videotape. He knows the defenses. He knows what he's gonna face night in and night out. He's not a dumb person at all when it comes to basketball."

So this Rodman thing still has great potential, all the elements of an impossible love story. The Spurs can't live with him and can't live without him. Robinson and Rodman, on the same roster. Sharing the same crazy neighborhood. Robinson works patiently and Rodman does drive bys.

It's just the kind of scenario that has everyone wondering what'll happen next.

FROM ENSIGN TO ADMIRAL

By now, Robinson should be used to dealing with bizarre, unforeseen events. Most NBA superstars spend their lives preparing for the day they'll have to carry big pressure and cash big checks. But for him, the path to the NBA was a short, strange trip.

Because his father was a career Navy man, Robinson suddenly found himself transferring to Osbourne Park High School in Northern Virginia just before the start of his senior year in 1982. Almost as an afterthought he went out for the basketball team that November, and although the coach had already made final cuts, he agreed to add the 6-6 newcomer.

Robinson had played basketball at his previous school in Virginia Beach, but sports made up only a small segment of his interests growing up. He spent much of his time completing electronics projects or practicing music or reading science fiction.

He figured he'd have a bright future, but sports hardly seemed to be a big part of it. Yet he was tall and played well enough his senior year at Osbourne Park to get the attention of coaches at the United States Naval Academy and Virginia Military Institute. He almost chose VMI but at the last moment settled on Navy, which he entered in the summer of 1983. "When I got there, I was about 6-7 and weighed about 185 pounds," he recalled. "One of the newspapers there said I looked like a swizzle stick in a blender."

Amazingly, he was in the midst of a pituitary explosion, growing 15 inches over six years. Even more amazing, the growth wasn't accompanied by joint problems, clumsiness or other side effects.

If Robinson was the swizzle stick, then Navy coach Paul Evans was the blender, a tough-minded sort who pushed his big men through brutal rebounding drills. "My freshman year was the toughest," Robinson said. "I wasn't really that interested in the basketball. It was kind of a task to come out there and do the work everyday.

"Evans was a tough guy, a good coach for me to start off with because he pushed me, really pushed me."

Robinson's growth continued to explode that year, and the media quickly took note of Navy's talented young freshman. That summer, he played abroad on a team of college stars that included Dell Curry and Chuck Person. "They kept telling me I was a real good player," he recalled. "I had never really thought of myself as being very good. They kept telling me I had a lot of skills and could be really good."

As his height neared seven feet, Robinson slowly began to see that his future might not be that of a career Navy officer. "For the first time," he

A PRISONER IN MR. ROBINSON'S NEIGHBORHOOD

said, "I realized, 'Hey, if I get my act together and start to play, maybe I could be pretty good.'"

In an amazing transformation over three seasons, he became the "Admiral," a dominating presence in the center of Navy's attack. He evolved from a little known college recruit to All-American and the top pick in the 1987 NBA draft, the only problem being that he had to serve two years in the Navy to fulfill his obligation from the Academy.

The Spurs, meanwhile, sank to a miserable 21-61 in 1989 while waiting for Robinson to join them. But he made the delay worthwhile, charging in to average 24.3 points, 12 rebounds, 3.89 blocks and 2 assists to win the 1990 Rookie of the Year award.

Bolstered by his arrival, the Spurs posted a 56-26 record and won the Midwest Division crown, the greatest one-year turnaround in league history. In 1992, Robinson was named the league's Defensive Player of the Year and has been an All Star in each of his five seasons, major accomplishments for a young man who entered college thinking his future lay in missle systems.

"It's a big change," he says of his transformation. "I never would have guessed that this is where I'd be. It's funny that I ended up here. I see all of my old friends, and they ask me what it's like. It doesn't seem that much different to me than the way it was before, except there's all this stuff surrounding me now. There's all the attention, all the lights, all the money and everything.

"But it's like...," he pauses here, searching for a metaphor, a way of explaining it. "It's like it's happening around me, and I just kind of enjoy it. I'm watching it. It's kind of fun. But, uh, I don't know. It's a little bit strange."

A player who takes being a role model seriously, Robinson doesn't mind revealing that he has a few of his own. Because both are deeply religious, it seems logical that Robinson would pick A.C. Green of the Phoenix Suns as his favorite. Green, after all, managed to keep his virginity intact while playing nearly a decade with the Los Angeles Lakers, a team famous for the sexual excesses of its stars. While Magic Johnson made a game of sleeping with an estimated 300 women per year, Green spent his off hours quietly reading scripture, even taking his Bible on the team bus.

"He's just a tremendous example," Robinson says of Green. "He's been doing it for a lot of years, and he's just a great worker. He's probably the guy I admire most."

From a pure basketball standpoint, Robinson shares idols with a zillion 12-year-olds. "Everybody," he says, "looks at a guy like Michael Jordan and you want to figure out what it was that enabled him to take his team to the top. He's one of the guys I look at and say, 'I'd like to have that kind of drive, that kind of intensity, because he's head and shoulders above everybody else.' That's something that goes through my mind: How do you attain that level?"

That, of course, is the modern NBA challenge, and perhaps no player is better suited to meet it than big Dave. His intelligence and faith have allowed him to outthink the circumstances. After all, isn't that the real secret? To work hard and bide your time, relentlessly bettering the circumstances with your effort and patience?

Along with that, Robinson believes he is playing for far more than a championship. He badly wants his fans to see that he is a regular guy, not caught up in the money and bright lights of stardom.

"What I do out here at this stage of my life is my ministry," he says. "I feel like when I come out here to play, I don't play for my own glory. I don't play for the statistics, the money. All that stuff is not nearly as important as showing people you can walk strong; you can have the temptations of the money; you can have the temptations that are around you; but you can be a great father, a great husband and just a strong man. You don't have to succumb to all the pressures. You don't have to become a jerk just because everybody is around you all of the time. It's a real special opportunity. I feel like God has put me in a special place. It's a lot of pressure. I take a lot of criticism and a lot of scrutiny.

"And I like it."

These last lines he says with all the enthusiasm his spirituality can muster, which is quite a bit. The less religious members of the Spurs staff are amazed, and perhaps a bit frightened, of Robinson's abiding faith.

If Robinson has a fault, says Glenn Rogers, who covers the team for the *San Antonio Express-News*, it's that he's oddly naive. In other words, his religion allows him to make leaps of faith that others simply can't, or shouldn't. It's what allows him to continue believing in a Dennis Rodman long after other people have switched off the lights.

Robinson doesn't find it ironic that others see his strength as a potential weakness. "Right now I'm doing exactly what I'm supposed to be doing," he says, "and I know the Lord's pleased with it."

Asked if he has ever contemplated the parallel life he might have led had he never grown to seven feet and become a star, Robinson stops. "No, not really," he says. "Personality wise, I think I'd be a lot different. I think basketball has taught me a lot about life, taught me a lot about how to carry myself. The success I've had has made me mature in a lot of ways."

He stops a moment and laughs. "Plus my wife has made me mature in a lot of ways."

Indeed, his 1992 marriage to Valerie changed his life dramatically, and some say, lessened his basketball drive, a factor that Robinson seemingly admits. Yet he sees religion and family as the solutions to the cold life of the NBA, not the complicating factor others claim it is. In fact, what Robinson so admired about Lucas was the coach's ability to establish a family atmosphere for the team in the midst of the very cynical business of pro sports. Not surprisingly, he sees his wife and child as a refuge. "It's great to have a family now," he says. "A couple of years ago when I didn't have a family, it was hard outside of basketball to find what you really wanted to do. Now it's easier. I spend time with my wife and baby.

"Before it was much harder. Basketball was always the center of things. You were out doing different stuff, but it always came back to the game."

He understands the long, empty hours that can drive young players to distraction, causing them to seek refuge in drugs and alcohol. He remembers the same feelings his first few years in the league. "You get restless. You want to do something. You want to find people to hang out with. I think that's the time when you choose the wrong people, do the wrong things, just because of your restlessness, because you don't really have any kind of home situation. You just travel and do the basketball things."

Which makes him all the more determined to be a role model for younger players. He looks to his religious teammates, Avery Johnson and Terry Cummings, and assistant coach Paul Pressey for help in these situations.

"I really feel like people who are walking strong with Christ are really strong characters," he says. "A guy like Avery is a strong person. He's a competitor; he's a warrior. I hope that kind of attitude rubs off. That's important. These other guys have to feed off our strength and our consistency and commitment."

The absolute center of Robinson's spiritual life is his family, particularly David Maurice Robinson, Jr., his two-year-old son. "I think

I've probably learned as much about God through my son as anything, any experience I've ever had," he says. "Obviously my relationship with my wife is the most special one, but he comes really, really close to that. He's like a mirror image of me, and I feel such a tremendous responsibility because he doesn't know anything. I didn't know how to be a father at first, but he's such a joy. I raise him. I teach him. It really gives me an understanding of how God looks at me and says, 'Man, you don't know anything. Just take your time, and I'll teach you what you need to know.'

"I look at my son the same way and say, 'Son, I have a lot for you. It's in store for you. Right now you're not ready for it. But when you mature, you'll be ready for it. I have great things.' And that's what God says to us. He says, 'David, you're not ready for it right now. But I've got some great things in store for you. Just wait until you mature and you grow up and inherit the whole shebang. You'll love it!'"

Yes, I think, this intensity could put people off a bit, particularly if they're not operating on the same spiritual wavelength. But, as Terry Cummings points out, the Spurs who hold deep religious convictions are careful not to foist Jesus on their teammates.

Still, Robinson's beliefs make me wonder about his politics. So I ask, and find out that, like many Americans, his view of the public arena emanates from his sense of family. "People think that the government can solve a lot of problems, and the government is already too big," he says. "In order to protect peoples' rights and the communities, families have to be strong. Communities have to be strong, not governments. For me, I'm real strong on family and real strong on community, but I'm not big on politics.

"I guess you'd call me religious right. I'm just very scriptural. I believe the Lord has all the sovereignty. I tend to be more conservative than anything else. I just don't like some of the things a lot of the liberals say nowadays. It's just too much for me. I don't believe in all these human rights things. I believe you've got to sacrifice for the good of the whole. It's nice to have some rights, but it just gets crazy after a while. It just gets ridiculous."

This sounds almost as if he's directing his comments at Rodman. But the power forward, who spends most of his time around the team with his head stuffed between a set of stereo headphones, probably wouldn't listen anyway.

That evening in a scrimmage, Moses Malone and Rodman square off. It's mostly woofing and posturing, and their teammates quickly separate them. The two local refs hired to run the scrimmage smile afterward and confide that they might have stepped in between the two big lugs if the pay had been a little better.

A PRISONER IN MR. ROBINSON'S NEIGHBORHOOD

I laugh and prepare to depart. My first interviews are over and now I'm free at last, paroled from Mr. Robinson's neighborhood. I'll gladly leave Kerrville and its stuffed, severed heads in my rearview mirror.

A week later, I catch up with the Spurs in Nashville, where they are scheduled to meet the New York Knicks in an exhibition game. Last year, a local investors group, led by Gaylord Entertainment, attempted to purchase the Minnesota Timberwolves and move them to Tennessee, a plan that failed. Regardless, the folks in Nashville still believe they have a chance at an NBA franchise. They view this exhibition game, at Vanderbilt University, as an opportunity to show the NBA they can support a team here. Accordingly, the league and Gaylord Entertainment, the promoters, have shaken the locals down with ticket prices that range from $30 to $50, even $60 and $70. Thinking they'll get to see the Admiral and New York's Patrick Ewing in action, the fans gladly shell out, only to find that Ewing is in street clothes. And while Robinson dresses out, he does not play because of tendinitis in his knees.

Rodman, however, does appear, and his hair is dyed a bright fuchsia, which provides at least a chuckle for the fans. The Spurs seem out of shape, and the Knicks easily control the game. Midway through the second half, the sellout crowd begins chanting, "We want David! We want David!"

Robinson remains seated despite their pleas, and after the game seems embarrassed at having disappointed the fans. I find him sprawled on a locker room couch, with a smattering of local reporters questioning him.

"The crowd was chanting; they really wanted to see you play," says one guy with a pen and notebook. "Any reason you didn't play?"

"Well," Robinson says with a degree of timidity, "just my knee. It's been a little bit sore this week. I got a little bit of tendinitis in there and I hadn't been able to practice as much as I wanted to."

For someone who wants to seem like a regular guy, big Dave should have explained his absence a little better, I think. To prepare for the season, he had gone to Aspen, Colorado, two weeks before training camp opened to train in the altitude, which supposedly has benefits when the trainee comes back down to earth. "It was great," he said, "but the results only lasted about a week."

In fact, Robinson came into camp and ran into a coach determined to whip his players into shape so that they could execute the running game. Hill had planned to condition his team twice a day, but after the first morning session Robinson asked to be excused. Having your team leader beg off of conditioning wasn't the greatest way to begin camp, so Hill relented and eased up on the program.

Now, in this first exhibition game, the Spurs were clearly out of shape, and afterward Hill stood outside the locker room looking glum. I asked him if anything about Robinson had surprised him. "When he wants to turn it on and really run the floor, he can really have a presence, more than you think he can," he replies.

This seemed hardly a rapturous endorsement. Were the superstar and coach already at odds?

Inside the locker room, I ask Robinson if conditioning has become a mountain for him. "No," he says hesitantly. "I mean it's just about loving the game, loving what you gotta do. You gotta prepare yourself physically and mentally to play this game.

"If you don't, it's a tough game," he adds with a laugh. "Boy, you come out there and you're not ready to play. . . ."

The thought of this seems horrifying, but another writer interrupts with a question about Rodman's new look. Robinson smiles. "Let's just suffice it to say that I wouldn't wear that 'do, but I think it works for him. It's much better than the green was last year, and much better than the blue."

"What's your favorite color?" the writer asks.

"I don't know," Robinson says. "I think this looks pretty good on him. This fuchsia is definitely him."

In the next room, Rodman is dourly packing up his gym bag. I walk up and extend my hand. Dennis, I say. You remember me. I used to write a lot about the Pistons back when you guys won the titles.

He eyes my hand suspiciously and draws back. "I gotta go," he says.

"Just a few quick questions," I plead.

He shakes his head and says, "Later. I gotta go now."

With that, he turns and heads out a side door into whatever night Nashville has waiting for a tattooed, earring-wearing, fuchsia-headed giant.

A PRISONER IN MR. ROBINSON'S NEIGHBORHOOD

I look at my empty extended hand and feel very jilted. Time, of course, will reveal that I'm not alone. In fact, I'm just beginning to see a tiny little bit of what it's like to be big Dave Robinson. Empty handed in a bad neighborhood.

IF YOU REMOVE ALL THE FRUITS AND FLAKES, YOU STILL GOT THE NUTS

Perhaps we should thank Charles Barkley and Dennis Rodman for reminding us that playing pro basketball has always involved more than, well, just playing basketball. To capture the public's attention, pro hoops has always relied on a certain zaniness, a certain outrageousness in its players. If anything, players like Barkley and Rodman are merely upholding a long-standing tradition.

Nothing demonstrates this better than the fact that the first practice facility of the old Minneapolis Lakers back in 1946 was a community center on the city's northwest side affectionately known as "The Nuthouse."

That was good, recalled the late Jim Pollard, a Hall of Famer and star for those old Lakers, because back then you had to be a bit loony to play pro basketball.

From the game's early days in 1896, pro hoopsters had played with fearlessness. They were competitive, hard-driving men. After Dr. James Naismith invented basketball at a YMCA training school in late 1891, the sport spread rapidly through the YMCA's network of clubs. Many early pros had first played the game on YMCA teams and become quite good at it. The better they played, the more they wanted to play. This, in turn, led to conflicts with YMCA officials over the use of the gym. Basketballers wanted to play all the time. And when the YMCA said no, the players went elsewhere, to local armories or Masonic temples or hotel ballrooms. Any place would do, just so long as it had a high ceiling and decent lighting.

To pay for the building, the players had to charge admission, which meant they were no longer amateurs, a scandalous development to

Victorian sensibilities. Pro basketballers were quickly labeled as outcasts. A YMCA official wrote in 1898 that "when men commence to make money out of sport it degenerates with tremendous speed. It has inevitably resulted in men of lower character going into the game."

Addicted as they were, the early players paid this condescension little mind. While money was a motivation, it wasn't the force that drove the first pros. Basketball was too risky a venture for that. Most who played and promoted it needed day jobs to get by. Still, the pro game grew steadily, and within a few decades the very biggest stars could pull down $2,400 a year, about three times the earnings of the average laborer. Still, the vast majority of early players made little or nothing. And their game remained a stepchild as leagues and franchises sprang to life across the Northeast, flowered briefly, then died. The surviving teams were mostly barnstormers who traveled about the country playing the locals. These early pros saw basketball as it was played in every region, and they incorporated the best ideas into their styles. They developed quick, short passing offenses and ran them off the post, an innovation that quickly found its way to the college game. Joe Lapchick, an early pro who later coached St. John's and the New York Knickerbockers, described this snappy passing style as "making the ball sing."

The first pro club, The Trenton New Jersey Basketball Team, formed in 1896. They wore velvet shorts with tights and played their home games at the local Masonic temple. After a few games, the team manager, a carpenter named Fred Padderatz, strung chicken wire around the Masonic temple court to keep the ball in play. Supposedly, Padderatz built it in response to an editorial comment in the *Trenton Daily True American* that "the fellows play like monkeys and should be put in a cage."

Within a few seasons the "cage" was the standard for pro games, although college coaches sneered at it. From Padderatz's chicken wire there developed a system of rope and wire cages draped about the court, some strung 15 to 20 feet high for keeping the ball in play. Thus basketball came to be known as the "cage game" and its players the "cagers."

The cage frequently resulted in wicked injuries and burns as players hurled themselves against it going after loose balls. Fans were said to be fond of poking knitting needles, lighted cigarettes, and other prods through the netting. In some Pennsylvania mining towns, spectators took to heating nails and tossing them onto opponents shooting free throws.

Soon other YMCA teams sought to match Trenton's success, which brought the rapid spread of "cager" teams throughout New England, New York, Pennsylvania and New Jersey. Unlike the college game, which disdained the continuous dribble, early pro rules allowed players to take a series of two-handed, single-bounce dribbles. As a result, the game had a rough nature, what you might call "the original ugly," with broad, hulking men dominating the ball up and down the floor, forcing their way near the goal to score. Head-on collisions were numerous, particularly in the small gyms of the era, many of which presented other obstacles, such as hot stoves, steam pipes, and even posts in the middle of the floor supporting the roof. (Legend has it that the posts in middle of the Trenton YMCA floor led to the original idea of "post" play.)

The "cage" game died in the 1920s, but pro basketball steamed on, as a series of leagues rose and fell. Any stability came from the great teams: Harlem's Renaissance Big Five, an all-black team better known as the Rens; the Original Celtics, a New York club that garnered wide attention; and the Philadelphia SPHAs, the South Philadelphia Hebrew Association team run by Eddie Gottlieb. Despite the inconsistency of the leagues, these teams survived because they barnstormed, playing as many as 200 games per season.

By the early 1930s, some basketball promoters found they could attract a decent crowd if they combined the games with a dance afterward, the only problem being that sometimes the "fans" were more interested in the dance. It wasn't unusual to have women in heels interrupt play with an inadvertent stroll across the floor. Back then, the game was played in three periods. The pros would play a period, then the fans would dance awhile. Then the pros would play another period. A popular venue was the old Broadwood Hotel in Philadelphia, a nightspot for Jewish singles, where the SPHAs played. "The floor was slick, a lot of dance wax on it," recalled Robert "Jake" Embry, owner of the old Baltimore Bullets. "The players were used to sliding and shooting. They'd dribble, slide about five feet, and shoot."

Very ugly.

During the late 1930s and '40s, pro basketball organized itself around the *Chicago Herald American* tournament. Each year, all the country's good pro teams, regardless of what league they played in, would meet in Chicago to settle who was best. Known simply as the "world tournament," the competition helped build public interest in the game. It was the place where the great early black teams, the Rens, the Washington Bears, the Harlem Globetrotters, were free to take on the all-white clubs, with the best men winning.

But, as fascinating as it was, the tournament couldn't do much to make pro basketball a stable business or change the lot of the average player. Like the pros in Trenton a half-century earlier, the teams of the 1940s still sported fancy uniforms (the rave was satin). Yet the day-today life of the players was a bit ragged. Training methods were minimal. At home, the teams usually employed a trainer of sorts, "but on the road, each guy took a roll of tape with him," said George Senesky, who played in the forties. "You knew how to tape your own ankles."

And as nice as the jerseys looked, there was no such thing as a clean road uniform. "You couldn't wash them; they had to be dry-cleaned," Senesky said. "On the jerseys, you could see the salt marks on them after a while. You had to hang it up in your room after the games so it would dry out. There was no equipment manager. You were responsible. But nobody complained about it. We were so glad to have the opportunity, so glad to be there."

Which makes you wonder why.

But as Les Harrison, owner/coach of the Rochester Royals, used to say, "This is still better than carrying a lunch bucket every day."

Out of an average $3,000 salary, a player would take home about $2,000. "A lot of us always thought it was going to get better the next year," Senesky said. "The best ticket was $2.50, and 50 cents of that was tax. The owners weren't making money either."

The shaky finances contributed to pro basketball's goofy image. In short, the whole game was a "nuthouse." You had to love it to play it. And then, as George Senesky pointed out, you often wondered why you did.

THE SCREAM TEAM

Despite the dramatic financial gains made by the modern game, the atmosphere around the sport retains that strong element of wackiness even today, despite the best efforts of the NBA's legions of publicity people who work to smooth out the wrinkles. Our high-flying pro hoops stars can be admired for many qualities, but mental stability usually isn't among them.

Yessir, it seems the wilder they are the better we like 'em. What else could account for the rampant popularity of the Barkleys and Rodmans of the world? Not only are they good, they're good 'n crazy. And they follow in the game's long and glorious line of wackos. If you wanted, I could even arrange some of the most notorious examples into an All-Star team, the Scream Team, if you will, the greatest nuts in the history of the game, all neatly arranged on a single roster for your reading pleasure. A number of them have gone on to that great rubber Ramada in the sky. As for those who are still living, please be cautious when asking for autographs. Some of these guys still have a bite!

Red Auerbach,
Coach and general manager

The legendary coach and general manager of the Boston Celtics has a long and glorious history of irrational behavior. Just as his Celtics were about to meet the St. Louis Hawks in the 1957 NBA Finals in St. Louis, Auerbach punched out Hawks owner Ben Kerner.

It seems the two were disagreeing over the height of the baskets. "Bennie went up to argue with him, and Red hit him in the mouth," veteran NBA scout Marty Blake recalled with a chuckle.

"He bloodied my lip," Kerner said. "You have to know Red. It was his style."

"I was talking to the refs," Auerbach explained, "and he interrupted me."

Thirty years later, Auerbach was in his 60s and still known for charging onto the court in fits of anger. In a 1987 preseason game against Philadelphia, he jumped up from his seat in the stands at Boston Garden and tried to punch 'Sixers center Moses Malone.

But Auerbach's worst offenses by far have come from behind the wheel. In the old days, the Celtics would travel by car, and no one would ride with speedy Red. Longtime Boston sportswriter Sam Brogna recalls that Auerbach had a favorite trick — letting the rest of the team leave 15 minutes ahead of him, then still beating everybody to the destination.

Dick Motta
Assistant coach

Although he's mellowed a bit with age, anyone who has played under Motta knows how tightly wrapped he is. NBC analyst Matt Guokas played for Motta with the Chicago Bulls in the 1970s. Guokas and several other Bulls recall one night Motta became so incensed that he spit on the ball and shoved it into the referee's hands.

"He used to kick the sign in front of the scorer's table and put dents in it," longtime Bulls scorekeeper Bob Rosenberg said of Motta. "One time referee Jack Madden gave him two technicals, then gave him a third for spitting on the ball and handing it back to him. He ended up that game with four technicals, but that's when they changed the rule. In those days, you could get three or four technicals and still not get kicked out. So they changed the rule. Motta did not like to lose."

Goukas recalled it this way: "Jerry Sloan, Chicago's great guard, was arguing with Jack Madden. We were going to a time out, and the ball was rolling toward Dick. Dick has gigantic hands. He was able to palm it. He picked the ball up with his left hand. He was kind of looking at the ball and feeling it and he was walking out to Jack Madden. Right before he handed it to him, he laid a big one on the ball and Jack didn't really see him spit on the ball. But when he had it in his hands, Jack knew Dick had spit on it."

"When Motta went into this other dimension he was liable to do anything," recalled veteran Chicago sportswriter Bob Logan. "I remember the night he drop-kicked the ball into the upper deck at Cobo Arena."

"The play happened right in front of our bench," Bob Weiss, a former Bulls guard, remembered. "Dick just caught the ball and took two steps like a punter and kicked the ball into the upper deck and sat down. One referee was breaking up a skirmish, and the other one was telling the scorer's table who the foul was on. So neither of them saw the kick. And now Dick Motta is sitting down and the refs are looking for the ball. And Detroit coach Butch Van Breda Kolff comes storming down the court yelling, 'He kicked the ball!!! He kicked the ball!!!' The officials don't know what the heck he's saying, so they gave him a technical. I think Van Breda Kolff got two technicals and was kicked out of the game. Meanwhile, there's two guys playing catch with the ball in the balcony. They finally got it down."

Jerry Sloan still laughs about the incident. "Van Breda Kolff got kicked out of the game for being upset because the officials didn't know who did it," he said. "Meanwhile, Motta's sitting there on the bench like nothing ever happened."

Kevin "Chuck" Connors
Forward

The late Connors was a reserve forward with the Celtics in 1946, then went on to fame as "The Rifleman" on the long-standing TV series. Some thought that Connors seemed a little light in the loafers during his playing days because he was fond of publicly reciting poetry ("Casey at the Bat" was one of his favorites). His communication skills obviously outranked his hoops prowess. After the Celtics released him, Connors turned to selling life insurance and talked his way into traveling with the team so that he could ink eager fans to a policy.

Fortunately, sales weren't too good and Connors went on to his career in television.

"The Rifleman," by the way, was the first NBA player to shatter a backboard, which he did just before the Celtics' very first game in 1946. One version of the story had him hanging on the rim, another said he shattered the glass with a bricklike bank shot.

Either way, Connors reigns as the grandaddy of all smashers.

Bill Russell
Center

People think that Rodman is strange today with his dyed hair and tattoos. But Russell, the great Celtic rebounder and shotblocker, was given to bizarre costumes in his day. He often wore capes and derbies and carried a cane. One night he showed up at the Garden dressed as Little Lord Fauntleroy, and the gate guard, claiming not to recognize him, refused to let him in the building.

Ray Felix
Center

Felix was named the league's Rookie of the Year in 1954, but he had little offensive skill and spent most of his career as a utility rebounder and defender. He played center for the Lakers in their early sixties battles against the Celtics. In one game, he took four shots and Celtics center Bill Russell blocked all four. On a fifth try, Felix backed in and tried to surprise Russell by flipping a shot over his shoulder. The ball sailed over the backboard. Felix then pointed at Russell and yelled, "You didn't get that one, baby!"

"Bill looked at him like, 'You're crazy, Ray,'" recalled Lakers teammate Hot Rod Hundley.

"He had strange habits," Hundley added. "Like he'd eat his dessert before he ate the rest of the meal. We called him Baby Ray because he called everybody Baby."

His teammates loved to see Felix pull up a chair to the card table. In hi-lo poker he always seemed to get confused and call a low hand when he had hi winners.

The Lakers narrowly lost Game 7 of the 1962 NBA Finals to the Celtics. Afterward, Felix sat in the lockerroom and consoled his teammates. "That's all right," he said. "We'll get 'em tomorrow."

Reggie Harding
Forward

Sadly, Harding was raised on Detroit's mean streets and could never overcome his gangster background. Although he never played in college, he was drafted by the Pistons and played for parts of two seasons with Detroit and Chicago. He was known for finishing practice and leaving without showering, pausing only to towel off and spin the cylinder on his revolver.

One night teammate Flynn Robinson awakened in the dark, cut on the light and found Reggie pointing a gun at him. Another time, Harding apparently began shooting at teammate Terry Dischinger's feet to make him 'dance.'

Legend has it that Harding, at 6-11, once donned a ski mask and robbed a grocery store in his own neighborhood.

The clerk said, "I know that's you Reggie."

"No, it ain't me, man," Reg replied. "Shut up and give me the money!"

The Chicago Bulls signed Harding in 1967. "We needed a big center," explained former Chicago coach Johnny Kerr. "I had heard about his pistol. Rumor had it that he carried it in his gym bag... He'd play one-on-one with Flynn Robinson. Flynn would beat him, and Reggie would say, 'Get out of here, Flynn, before I pistol whip you.' Everybody figured he might have it with him.

"When we were in the midst of a losing streak in '67, we played the Lakers in Los Angeles. We needed a win in the worst way, and we had a one-point lead with just a few seconds left on the clock. The Lakers got the ball at half court, and I put Reggie in to guard Mel Counts, their big guy. I didn't want them getting an alley-oop. Counts set up out near the free throw line, but Walt Hazzard, who was taking the ball out of bounds, threw the ball over the backboard and the buzzer sounded. I was jumping around and screaming because we had finally won a game. I looked up, and Reggie had decked Mel Counts. Counts got up and shot two free throws and beat us."

A few days later, the Bulls released Harding.

Darryl Dawkins
Center

Dawkins, who left high school in Florida and went directly to the Philadelphia 76ers in 1975, is legendary for his zaniness. He, too, like Chuck Connors was a backboard smasher, but there was little doubt as to how Dawkins accomplished his destruction. He tore backboards down with his monster slams and referred to himself and his dunking prowess as "Chocolate Thunder." As charming as he was crazy, Dawkins liked to tell reporters he was from the planet "Lovetron."

In the 'Sixers' 1977 NBA Finals showdown with the Portland Trailblazers, Dawkins got sidetracked in a physical battle with Portland's Maurice Lucas. Their fighting took the young Dawkins out of his game and enabled the Blazers to win.

"I lost my funk," Dawkins explained afterward.

Charlie Yelverton
Guard

Yelverton only played the 1971-72 season with Portland, but that was all he needed to establish his legend. Kareem Abdul-Jabbar once described him as the "NBA's only black hippie."

Yelverton wore dreadlocks and was said to use bales of marijuana as furniture in his apartment. For pregame warm-ups, he went to midcourt and meditated.

Hot Rod Hundley
Guard

Like Laker legend Jerry West, Hundley played college basketball at West Virginia University, where rumor has it that coach Fred Schaus was so conscious of "image" that he required his players to shave their armpits.

The first pick of the 1957 draft, Hundley was another of the NBA's legendary partiers and cardplayers. At one point, Minneapolis Lakers owner Bob Short became so frustrated with Hundley's carousing that he offered to have women sent to Hundley's room, in hopes that Hundley might actually turn in early and get some sleep before a game.

Hot Rod, however, declined, telling Short, "The thrill is in the chase, baby."

Later, when the Lakers moved to Los Angeles, Hundley became known as a clown who thrilled crowds with his dribble-king showboat routine late in blowout games. Hundley liked to infuriate the other team by shooting hook shot free throws.

He was very fond of actress Doris Day, who sat courtside in the L.A. Sports Arena. He'd pull up his dribble in front of her seat, give her a wink and toss up a 30-foot hook shot.

Dave Cowens
Center

It was funny that San Antonio would hire Dave Cowens in 1994 to help coach Dennis Rodman. When Cowens played for the Celtics in the 1970s, he, too, was known as a free spirit. Once, he dropped off the team for a while and starting driving a taxi. But when he played, he played center with the force and lateral quickness of a linebacker. "I don't worry about injuries," he once said. "I'm the one going a little bit nutty out there. I don't get hit because I'm the one doing the hitting."

He invested in a catfish farm in Honduras and became so involved in an auto mechanics course that Auerbach asked him to drop it.

Marvin Barnes
Forward/center

Barnes was a bonus baby for the old St. Louis Spirits of the American Basketball Association who favored gobbling down steak, potatoes, nachos, or anything, in the locker room just minutes before taking the floor for a game. A prodigious talent given to wearing mink coats, driving expensive cars and escorting a woman on each arm, Barnes bolted from the Spirits just 17 games into his pro career and was later found in a Dayton, Ohio, poolroom, caught up in a marathon game.

He was rumored to have 13 phones in his six-room apartment. He missed dozens of appearances, flights and games during his tenure with the Spirits and once explained that he was late to practice because he lost his car downtown. What kind of car do you drive? his coach asked. "A Bentley," Barnes replied.

Charles Barkley
Forward

In today's media intensive climate, all you need to do is mention Sir Charles' name to get a knowing nod from fans. Barkley has talked of running for the governor of Alabama after his playing days are over. Instead, he might want to check with Darryl Dawkins about the possibility of assuming the presidency of Lovetron. See Chapter Five.

Dennis Rodman
Forward

See Chapter Seven.

Dave Corzine
Center

Bulls center Will Perdue recalled that Corzine once showed up for a three-day roadtrip with a sweatsuit and a briefcase, and that he proceeded to wear the sweatsuit for three days.

One of the NBA's true "animals," Corzine is legendary around the league for passing gas. In fact, late, great referee Earl Strom once threatened to throw big Dave out of a game if he broke wind again. It seems Strom was going to charge Corzine with playing a zone defense.

Fly Williams
Guard

He played college ball at Austin Peay, where legend has it, he lay down on the floor in the middle of a game because he was angry the refs wouldn't give him a call. Playing for the St. Louis Spirits, he once got in a fight with one of his own teammates during pregame layup drills.

Because he had no teeth, the Spirits encouraged him to get dental work, but Williams was terrified of dentists. So he missed his appointment. When team officials asked about it, Williams replied, "Man, if I had teeth, I wouldn't be Fly."

THE DREAM CONFERRED
NOVEMBER, 1994

He used to be a lukewarm Muslim, but in recent years 31-year-old Hakeem Abdul Olajuwon has discovered the peace of a moral, contemplative lifestyle. He spends his Fridays at the Mosque praying. Despite his millions, he lives simply, studying the Koran and falling five times each day to face Mecca, seeking absolution and harmony and a deeper relationship with Allah.

When Hakeem gives a friend a gift, it's usually a prayer rug. When he chides an NBA official for a bad call, he never uses profanity. When he answers questions, he proceeds thoughtfully, producing insights at nearly every turn in the conversation.

Of course his life hasn't always flowed so transcendently. The old Olajuwon, then known as Akeem the Dream, was sometimes considered selfish and petulant, just like so many other rich, talented, young NBA stars. He seemed determined not to pass the ball away from the double- and triple-teaming defenses that neutralized him. Even worse, he seemed destined to waste the best years of his career bickering with the Houston Rockets front office.

But that was then. He's older and wiser now, a picture of a man who has mastered himself and put away the past.

Or at least most of it.

He still loves jazz, almost as much as he did in his wanton youth.

You can see that most any game night if you squeeze in among the throng in the Summit. There, just behind the home goal during warm-ups, will be a jazz band blaring away, filling the arena with brassy noise. On the floor nearby, Olajuwon, with the slightest smile twitching underneath his frowning game face, will be choreographing his spinning post moves. Like a dancer, he'll whirl with the ball cradled in his arm, pivoting first right, then left. He'll pause, facing the goal, to execute a jab step. Up and back. Leaning in with the ball pulled into his waist, waiting to launch his fallaway jumper over an imaginary opponent.

He stops only to dab at the sweat on his brow with the hem of his T-shirt.

Then he resumes whirling and pivoting, facing the basket then moving away, pausing to send his head fake flying before spinning suddenly into a 360. When he does this, he picks up his pivot foot. In college, that would be a walk. But this is Texas and the NBA, so the two-step is in vogue.

Besides, it's art, and if we hadn't witnessed Michael Jordan's many fancy flights, we just might consider Olajuwon the greatest artist of them all. Instead, it's his misfortune to follow in the shadow of the three stupendous championships won by Jordan's Chicago Bulls. Without a doubt, Hakeem's the most graceful big man to ever play the game. Yet grace isn't something that's on the minds of the critics these days. When Olajuwon himself finally reached championship status last season after a decade of trying, it seemed that all anyone could talk about was the absence of show and finesse with the Rockets and New York Knicks hammering away at each other in the 1994 NBA Finals. Never mind that Jordan himself often had to stoop to conquer the brutish Knicks, the chorus of complaints about a boring Finals obscured Olajuwon's superb 1994 performance. The championship series, after all, was butt ugly, particularly the physical defense and unimaginative offense provided by Pat Riley's Knicks.

In case you missed it, Olajuwon became the first player in NBA history to be named the Most Valuable Player of both the regular-season and the Finals and to claim the league Defensive Player of the Year award (although Bill Russell certainly should have garnered those honors several times over). For the fourth time in his decade-old career, Olajuwon ranked among the top 10 in four statistical categories. He finished second in blocked shots (3.71); third in scoring (a career-high 27.3 points per game); fourth in rebounding (11.9); and tenth in field goal percentage (.528).

While outstanding, this performance simply falls on top of Hakeem's remarkably consistent career. For nine consecutive seasons, he has finished with at least 100 steals and 200 blocks, a string unmatched in NBA history. (Houston fans, of course, would hasten to add that it's not just the quantity of Olajuwon blocks that they so cherish but the quality as well. Among the three times that one of his blocks assured a playoff win for the Rockets was the stuff of John Starks' shot in the closing seconds of the Finals critical Game 6.)

For his first 10 seasons in the league, Olajuwon has averaged better than 11 rebounds per game. Only Wilt Chamberlain (14 seasons), Bill Russell (13), Elvin Hayes (12), and Bob Pettit (11) have longer streaks, but that's because they played longer.

Barring something unforeseen, Olajuwon could press on to become the grandaddy of them all. Entering his 11th season, he's superbly conditioned and talks of playing forever.

"I play the game because I love the game," he says. "It's a form of exercise. If I weren't playing I'd worry about how I would keep my body in shape.

"Eat good, exercise, lift weights. So I don't buy into the premise of early retirement. Retire to what? What can you do better? There is mental stress in this job because you worry about the game. But that's the only work about it, the stress. The exercise and health aspects are fantastic. And beyond that, you have the competitiveness. It's a great job, a healthy job."

THE LAGOS LEGEND

His journey to this state of basketball bliss began in Lagos, Nigeria, in 1978, when at age 15, Olajuwon played hoops for the first time. The son of a businessman, Olajuwon thought he had found his calling as a soccer goalie. But Richard Mills, an American coaching Nigeria's national team, began campaigning for the young seven-footer to switch sports, saying he was too tall for soccer.

Olajuwon was swayed but almost got sidetracked in his first big game because he had no offensive skills. "I didn't know how to dunk," he explained. "And I didn't know how to lay it up either. I didn't know how to use the glass."

Frustrated, he almost quit, but his coaches kept talking up his potential. Then in 1980 he saw an Ebony magazine story on Kareem Abdul-Jabbar and Magic Johnson, who had just led the Lakers to the NBA title. The young African liked the sound of their names and was amazed by the star-quality of their status. That opened his eyes to basketball's promise.

"My coaches in Nigeria thought I could play competitively at the college level," he recalled. "So that was the ultimate goal, to go to school for free.

I just wanted to get my degree and either work here in the United States or go back to Nigeria."

According to an old story, he nearly enrolled at N.C. State or several other schools, but Olajuwon says his only choice was the University of Houston. On his first flight to this country in 1981, he landed for a brief stay in New York but quickly came to detest the traffic and cold weather and moved on to Texas.

After some mixed-up directions that almost took him to the University of Texas in Austin, Olajuwon's taxi dropped him on the steps of Houston's gym, where the African center would begin his stormy but productive relationship with legendary Cougars coach Guy Lewis. His coaching style seemed caustic and overly critical to the sensitive young Olajuwon, but no college coach in America was a better teacher of post play. And no coach better loved watching his players dunk.

In the young African, Lewis found the ultimate post student, although it didn't seem that way at first.

Fortunately, Olajuwon's parents owned a concrete business, and from that affluence, he had been able to gain a good education. He spoke French, English and four Nigerian dialects, which meant a relatively smooth off-court adjustment. On court was another matter.

"Olajuwon had played exactly four months of basketball when he came here," Lewis recalled. "That's not even equal to one full season of junior high ball...I don't mind telling you, when I first saw him play, I wasn't sure he could do it. He was 6'11". He could run and he could jump. But he knew absolutely nothing about basketball. And he couldn't shoot."

Olajuwon started only six games as a freshman and averaged 8.3 points, but he remained an unpolished sub who got most of his playing time in practice. "I go in, I get my five fouls and I go back to the bench," he said of that first year at Houston. "Coach Lewis keeps yelling at me, 'Akeem, stay on the floor.' Basketball wasn't fun."

He entered Houston's starting lineup for the 1982-83 season as a full-fledged member of the school's dunking fraternity, Phi Slama Jama, but in many game situations he was still unsure of what to do. "We really spent time working with all our post people," Lewis said. "I played the post myself and have always emphasized its importance. But after a year of working with Olajuwon, it still wasn't there yet."

Lewis remembered laughing early in the year, when reviewing a game videotape, he heard a TV announcer say that Olajuwon had learned his post moves by playing soccer in Africa. Soccer certainly provided Olajuwon the opportunity to develop excellent footwork, but the intricacies of playing the post were another matter. On raw talent alone, the center had some big offensive games early in his sophomore season, including 30 points against the University of Utah and 22 rebounds against SMU. But the tougher competition easily found ways of neutralizing him.

The breakthrough for Olajuwon didn't come until February. Houston had gone to Fort Worth to meet a tough Texas Christian team, and Olajuwon's picture was prominent in the local papers. The publicity irritated Lewis because Olajuwon was struggling while the rest of the team, led by Clyde Drexler, was playing well.

The center seemed lost against TCU, and late in the game, he had failed to score and had only one rebound. "Olajuwon was fouled and went to the line for two shots with a little time left and we were protecting a two-point lead," Lewis recalled. "The first shot hit the backboard like a rifle shot but somehow banked through. He missed the next one, but we held on and ended up winning. Olajuwon ended up with two points and one rebound, and I sarcastically told him he won the game for us.

"Then I told him he had gotten more publicity and done less than any player in the history of Houston basketball," Lewis said. "From that point, he seemed determined to show me. He just became dominating in practice."

His game performances weren't bad either. Houston became the first school to keep stats for dunks, and Olajuwon led Phi Slama Jama that season with 68 slams. Yet it was on the defensive end that he set himself apart with a school-record 175 blocks (5.1 per game). His intimidating presence allowed his Cougar teammates to gamble for steals (they averaged 11.4 per game).

Olajuwon's surge pushed Houston to the top of the college game, and that spring of 1983 the Cougars dominated the field in the NCAA tournament. Yet all of his personal progress seemed lost in the hoopla when N.C. State pulled one of the greatest upsets in tournament history, defeating Houston with Lorenzo Charles' last-second dunk, which left Lewis fuming to reporters that Olajuwon had failed to box out Charles.

Even with the defeat, Olajuwon was named the Final Four's Most Outstanding Player with 41 points, 40 rebounds and 19 blocks in two games.

Drexler turned pro after that season, but Olajuwon returned to take the Cougars back to the NCAA championship game yet again, this time for a loss to Patrick Ewing and the Georgetown Hoyas. Yet the Houston program's success and the high-profile losses established Olajuwon as the central figure in the city's complicated sports persona.

That spring of 1984, the Houston Rockets held the top pick in the NBA draft, and hoping that he would be their selection, Olajuwon decided to forego his senior year in college. Although the Rockets already had a Rookie-of-the-Year center in Ralph Sampson and Michael Jordan was also in the draft, the Rockets took Olajuwon and announced formation of the Twin Towers.

The move paid almost immediate dividends. With Sampson and Olajuwon presenting matchup problems for opponents around the league, the Rockets upset the Lakers and earned a spot against the Celtics in the 1986 NBA Finals. They lost in six games, a defeat that Olajuwon considers the most painful in his career, but hope for the future loomed large. Olajuwon figured he was part of a team that would come to rule over the NBA.

Instead, things fell apart. Sampson's knees went bad, and the Rockets traded him. Coach Bill Fitch was eventually fired, and the Rockets' front office never could seem to find a supporting cast of guards and forwards to play with Olajuwon. Four seasons of promise passed with no dividends.

Still, by 1991, things seemed on the upswing. Olajuwon had long established himself as the best center in the game. Otis Thorpe, obtained in a trade with Sacramento, had fit in nicely at power forward. And Don Chaney had replaced Fitch to drive the Rockets to a franchise-best 52 wins.

But fortunes swiftly plummeted in 1992. Olajuwon wanted a pay raise to bring his salary in line with the league's other superstars and soon found himself in a standoff with the front office. Then he injured his hamstring and missed several games. The team's doctor cleared him to play, but Olajuwon listened to a second medical opinion that said the injury needed more time to heal. The front office responded by accusing him of malingering to spur contract talks. Furious, Olajuwon demanded to be traded. The ensuing blowup cost the team its progress and Chaney his job.

Assistant Rudy Tomjanovich was promoted to replace Chaney, but the 1992-93 season opened under a cloud. On media day, Olajuwon told the press that the Rockets were being run by fools, that then-owner Charlie Thomas was a coward hiding behind then-General Manager Steve Patterson.

Fortunately, the Rockets faced a 14-hour plane ride for a game in Tokyo. On the trip, Olajuwon and Thomas talked out their differences. "When you are on a plane, you can run but you can't hide," Olajuwon said upon deplaning in Japan. "You can't get off and 14 hours is too long to spend locked in a bathroom."

The offshoot was a four-year, $25.4-million contract extension that paid Olajuwon on a level with the league's other centers. "It's a great day in Rockets history," Tomjanovich said with a huge smile. From there, the coach went to work convincing his center to pass out of the double- and triple-teams he faced.

In Olajuwon's defense, passing the ball hadn't always been his best option, considering the Rockets poor perimeter game. But Tomjanovich had remedied that by setting up an armada of three-point specialists around Olajuwon to make opponents pay for their double teams. "When the Rockets are hitting their threes, you might as well pack it up and go home," explained Phoenix forward Charles Barkley, "because you can't double-team Hakeem."

Houston made a nice run in the 1993 playoffs, then opened the next season by winning 18 of 19 games. With Jordan out of the league, the national press suddenly began noticing Olajuwon, prompting *Houston Chronicle* columnist Fran Blinebury to observe that Hakeem was "the elephant who has been standing smack in the middle of the living room for the past 10 seasons and is just beginning to get noticed by the experts sitting on the sofa."

The pain, however, was by no means over. The Rockets rolled into the 1994 playoffs and promptly lost their first two second-round home games to Phoenix, bringing the *Chronicle* to declare CHOKE CITY in its next morning's headlines, a reference to the city's long-suffering anguish over its sports teams' failure to produce in the clutch.

Earlier in the week, Olajuwon and guard Vernon Maxwell had lashed out at Houston fans for their lackluster support during a Sunday afternoon playoff game. This time, though, Olajuwon only commented that you can't tell about the character of a team when it's winning. You have to wait until times get tough.

Only one other team in NBA history, the 1969 Lakers, had come back after losing its first two games at home in a seven-game series. But with Olajuwon ruling the lane the Rockets caught the Suns and escaped with a seventh game victory in Houston.

From there, they went on to defeat the Knicks and eliminate thoughts of Choke City forever. That, unfortunately, hasn't resulted in all of the "respect" that Olajuwon and his teammates would like. They complain that both media and the fans consider their championship an anomaly, almost as if the Rockets snuck in and stole it when the rest of the basketball world was snoozing. Actually, though, most coaches and players around the league had long viewed Olajuwon as a slumbering giant, one that just about everybody hoped would stay asleep. Now, however, he has awakened to his prime.

"Now that Michael has left, Hakeem is the most complete player in the game — there's no doubt in my mind," says Cleveland center Brad Daugherty. "He's 31 years old, an age when you're considered to be on the downside of your career, but he's just exploded into the greatest player in the league."

For Olajuwon, that's only cause for more praise for Allah. These days when he jumps behind the wheel of his white Mercedes, he pops recorded verses from the Koran — not jazz — into the tape player. "It's beautiful for calm, for meditation, for peace," he explains. "When you pray to Mecca, you play the best music in the world."

BANK SHOTS: THE RISE OF DAVID STERN'S NBA

NOVEMBER, 1994

Michael Jordan's abrupt decision to retire from basketball has left a major vacuum in the league. Now that he's off taking minor league batting practice, many observers wonder, who's the best player in pro basketball? Who's the master of the game?

The answer to that one is certainly open to debate, but the top candidate has a wilting shot and probably couldn't jump over the Manhattan phone book without tripping.

Regardless, many will testify that NBA Commissioner David Stern is very much a player. He just might be the most competent, efficient executive in America.

Or the world, for that matter.

Many observers consider him the best commissioner in the history of American professional sport, better even than baseball's legendary Kenesaw Mountain Landis.

Of course you'd never know it just to look at him. He's got that pudgy, amiable exterior, sort of like pro basketball's Pillsbury Doughboy. He's endearingly clumsy enough to drop a trophy at a presentation now and then. Or he can flub his lines at a staged event like the NBA draft. But please don't let the faux pas fool you. Underneath that exterior, David Stern is a tough, street-smart competitor.

His education is as a lawyer, but his mindset runs to promotion and sales. In other words, he knows how to get to "Yes," and he's done it quite a few times for the NBA over the past decade. Since he became commissioner in 1984, the league has virtually bathed in a cash flow, a stunning 1,000 percent growth in annual revenues in 10 short seasons.

Asked about the explosion, Stern says, "Our players, they just happen to be the greatest athletes in the world. We have, by working together with them, managed to clear away a lot of things, the issue of drugs, the issue of renegotiations and collective bargaining, to clear away problems that allowed our fans to focus on our players.

"And each year, whether we're talking about Chris Webber or Anfernee Hardaway or Tony Kukoc or Gheorge Muresan, the influx of great players into the league is terrific.

"I think our owners deserve an extraordinary amount of credit, because they've made the investment in the teams, not just in the players, but the organizations. That's very important. People tend to focus on what the league has done. We get a lot of credit for the growth. But I hasten to point out that the teams have become important elements in their communities. Virtually all of our teams have community relations directors, public relations directors, kids programs, the kinds of things that you expect from good neighbors. And that's not lost."

Beyond the big stars and the beefed up PR, the growth of the NBA is basically attributable to the actualization of Stern's grand vision. Since becoming league commissioner in February 1984, he has relentlessly advanced the notion that the NBA is a "global entertainment company."

Now, there are signs all across the landscape that the world is buying into American professional basketball in a big way. One small example is that the league's promotional magazine, *HOOP*, is now being translated into Icelandic.

Icelandic?

"They came to us and wanted to get involved," Josh Rosenfeld, the NBA's director of international public relations, said of the Icelanders. That interest has spurred Norwegians to want their own edition, too.

Rosenfeld says there are approximately 170 countries that belong to FIBA, the international basketball organization, and that NBA games are now regularly broadcast in all of those countries.

Bogdan Stanculescu, a Romanian sports broadcaster, says that the NBA All Star Game is aired live in his country between 1 and 3 a.m. and draws a whopping 33 percent of the small country's audience. "Romanian kids," Stanculescu says, "know the NBA better than American kids."

Yet this isn't just a matter of bored Icelanders and captive Eastern Europeans. And it's not an accident. It's the result of a methodical global assault by the NBA that includes bringing international stars into the league, having NBA teams participate in international competition, and staging international exhibition games. These efforts are all part of Stern's master plan.

Central to the strategy, the NBA has made its television rights for most foreign countries very cheap, meaning that during the season video clips of Shaq and other NBA stars jamming and slamming are being shown nonstop around the globe (a frightening thought). "I don't want to say we give the games away," Rosenfeld says. "It's more that we take a minimal rights fee. The first time we go into a country, it's more to get exposure."

And that exposure has translated into thriving equipment and memorabilia sales. ("The NBA logo represents a real status symbol abroad," one league executive explained.) The annual gross sales of NBA merchandise around the globe is nearing $3 billion with international moneys accounting for approximately $500 million of that. Good as those foreign revenues appear, they represent only the tip of a vast potential that Stern wants to tap.

"It's where our growth is going to be," Rosenfeld says. "What David likes to talk about is that there are 260 million potential NBA fans in the United States. But there are three billion potential fans outside the U.S. He sees it as a matter of cutting down the borders.

"One of his favorite things, he'll ask you — and this is a typical David question — is, 'What do you know about India?' India is a country of a billion people that has a huge middle class. That's one of his fantasies."

To realize this dream, Stern has opened NBA satellite offices in Geneva, Hong Kong, Tokyo and most recently Mexico City (where he envisions a new franchise before the turn of the century). In August the league opened a Miami office to service Latin America, and next season the NBA hangs out a shingle in Canada with expansion teams in Vancouver and Toronto.

Germany, one of the traditionally toughest markets for the league to crack, has finally swooned, with regularly televised games and a growing media interest in the league. In February 1994, a throng of German journalists converged on the NBA All Star Game in Minneapolis (they were among more than 1,000 media representatives present), where one German TV crew asked Stern to explain his "great wish for basketball."

"The number one sport in the world," the commissioner said with an avuncular smile, "played by hundreds of millions of children around the world, just having a good time... A backboard, four to six kids wearing athletic shoes and having a good time, that's the best of basketball."

THE BAD OLD DAYS

When Jerry Zgoda began covering the NBA for the *Minneapolis Star Tribune* a few years back, he decided to research the recent history of the league for background. The first article he encountered was a 1983 *Newsweek* story that called the NBA "the sorriest mess in professional sports."

Indeed it was.

In 1980, the league's gross revenues were a pitiful $118 million, and 17 of its 23 teams were losing money as they watched player salaries spiral out of control. Team owners, who bickered constantly, contemplated the folding of four franchises. CBS thought so little of the NBA as a broadcast property that it didn't even air live the sixth game of the championship series between the Lakers and 76ers. (Yes, that marvelous championship performance of rookie Magic Johnson was sent to many parts of the country on late-night tape delay.)

Even worse than the finances was the cloud of scandal. By 1982, the *Los Angeles Times* estimated that 75 percent of the league's players were on drugs. Hotels around the league had become known as party palaces that drew regular crowds eager to greet the players as the teams came and went. "The marijuana smell, if you stayed one place in Oakland, it would keep you awake it was so pungent," former Lakers general manager Pete Newell said. "The place was wall-to-wall hookers. And the lounge was a nonstop party."

"I think we were in an awkward era for the league itself," Lakers executive Jerry West recalled. "It was floundering, and we didn't have any direction."

Fortunately for the NBA, the league's savior was already at work. As a partner in the firm of Proskauer Rose Goetz & Mendelsohn, Stern had been representing the NBA in court cases since 1967. Then in 1978, NBA commissioner Larry O'Brien convinced Stern to become the league's first full-time staff lawyer. In 1980, he was named the NBA's first executive vice president. His immediate job description was to beef up the league's public relations, broadcasting and marketing.

That wasn't easy.

Most Madison Avenue power players didn't have time to schedule meetings with NBA sales people, much less listen to how the league was going to change. "Our problem," Stern recalled, "was that sponsors were flocking out of the NBA because it was perceived as a bunch of high-salaried, drug-sniffing black guys."

Some observers saw the circumstances as racist, but Stern suggested there was opportunity. "It was our conviction," he explained at the time, "that if everything else went right, race would not be an abiding issue to NBA fans, at least not as long as we handled it correctly."

Handling it correctly meant a variety of Stern measures, the most important of which was the league's much-admired drug program. That was soon followed by a collective bargaining agreement and a salary cap.

The swiftness of the turnaround was stunning. By the 1983-84 season, the NBA set an attendance record (and would set eight more over the ensuing decade). That February of 1984, after O'Brien stepped down, the owners rewarded Stern by naming him commissioner. The timing matched the budding rivalry between Magic Johnson and Larry Bird and the arrival of Jordan, giving the NBA charismatic young stars to promote.

Still, much remained to be done. "You have to sell and sell and sell," Stern said at the time, summing up the challenge that faced him.

And litigate and litigate and litigate. As a lawyer, Stern learned to become a marketing genius. As a marketing genius, he remained a lawyer. The NBA has fought dozens of legal battles in his decade at the helm. With its players association. With the Chicago Bulls over cable television rights. With states and provinces to prevent legalized gambling from staining the integrity of the game.

And when Stern isn't litigating, he's using his toughness to advance the league's position. His wrath is legendary among network sports executives, particularly if they fail to show the NBA's best side. "He used to tell me he could run CBS Sports better than I," Peter Lund, the division's former president, once remarked.

Yet it's fair to say that Stern prefers charm over litigation or intimidation, a prime example of which was his soft touch in Minneapolis last February when local leaders and Timberwolves owners had begun insulting each other in the press over the team's future. "Stern was the unifying factor," Zgoda says. "He got everyone to sit down."

Minneapolis residents also watched him stare down Top Rank, Inc., and other moneyed interests from Louisiana that were intent on pulling the T-Wolves south. "You could see the power he has," Zgoda said of watching Stern shrug off threatened lawsuits by Top Rank.

The power, in part, stems from his special relationship with the league owners. Fearing that he was about to be stolen away by Major League Baseball in 1989, the owners gave him a whopping $27.5 million, five-year contract that included a $10-million bonus and a $3.5 million annual contract.

Although the fifth year of that deal has closed, Stern indicated last February that the agreement will roll over. "Even if I were on a handshake, my contract is like the Energizer," he said. "It just keeps going."

Certainly the 52-year-old Stern has any range of options available. In fact, if he were going to use his accomplishments as a stepping stone to baseball or some major corporate role, now would be the time to leave, with his brainchild in such solid shape.

Yet despite its overwhelming success, the NBA faces what Stern sees as substantial threats to the delicate balance he has created in the league. Foremost, the league must replace its primary star. Of Jordan's abrupt departure, Stern says, "I didn't think he was gonna do what he did. But I think it's great and I wish him well. I have no idea how he's gonna do (in baseball). I can't hit a curveball either. But he's the most extraordinary athlete I've ever seen."

This nonchalance is obviously studied because Jordan's stardom has lighted the league's path to financial health. Stern's job is to focus the fans' attention on younger stars while trying to pretend that Jordan's absence is just another coming and going in the cycle of pro sports. Ha.

The other major threats to the league include the negotiation of a new collective bargaining agreement and the paucity of revenue for the NBA's small-market teams. But really, all the battles that Stern fights for the NBA are connected. It's as if the league is a giant building, held together by high-tension, and Stern is the centerpiece that makes that tension work.

There is the tension of the big markets that could overpower the little markets if not for the salary cap that keeps the teams on something of a level court.

There is the tension between the owners and their greed. "They are short range," Utah Jazz executive Frank Layden says of pro sports owners. "They're not concerned with quality. They're concerned with the effective making of money. One owner said to me, 'We are not in the horse racing business.' Guys who own horses are constantly trying to better the breed; they're constantly trying to enhance the sport. In football, basketball and baseball, no, they are not trying to do that. They don't care, but somehow the game goes on without them and improves."

The two recent expansion teams in Canada each paid $125 million to join the league. The owners would like more of that easy money, would like to see more expansion, but how much dilution can the quality of play stand?

Finally, there is the tension between the owners and players over the salary cap. The collective bargaining agreement between the NBA and its players association ran out at the end of last season. The players had made it known for some time that they wanted to end the salary cap and the draft, to adopt what they call "an open-market" approach to player contracts.

Although they get 53 percent of certain league revenues, the players receive nothing from the sale of T-shirts and memorabilia. Thus they get little of the cash the league is raking in from overseas. The players want a taste of those monies.

The rhetoric about negotiations for the new contract was just starting to pick up earlier this summer when Stern launched a preemptive strike by filing a suit against the Players Association, asking the courts to bind them to the old contract until the new one could be negotiated.

Some critics charged that the NBA's suit pushed the borders of good legal taste, but the courts sided with the league. Which meant that the road was clear for the league to conduct its business and open the schedule again for the fall of 1994. But since the court rulings, the two sides have hardly spoken to one another, and the climate for discussions seems chilled.

Will the dispute lead to a strike in basketball, as it did in baseball?

That is just one of the questions troubling David Stern in what should be his hour of triumph.

In particular, he sees a tightening of network television revenues in the not-too-distant future. Which will put even more pressure on the tension between the big markets and little markets in the league.

"There are about to become some severe pressures on teams and localities where the revenue opportunities aren't as good as other places," Stern says. "What you need is a long-term strategy not to have your pockets emptied.

"I have a concern as a league about the viability of markets, as revenues skyrocket and as things come into play like local cable revenue."

He notes that in baseball network TV revenue has gone down, putting increased pressure on teams in smaller cities, like Pittsburgh. "So local revenue becomes more important," he says. "If you're in a small market, you've got a serious problem. In the absence of network revenue, you've got to focus on what you can do locally."

The tough solution is to help small market teams manage their affairs well and pick up extra revenue from promoting music concerts, hockey, arena football or whatever will help fill the building on off nights. Stern likes to brag that the NBA is a collection of "27 theme parks."

For some owners, the easy solution for the league is to keep raking in the money from expansion. But already critics, such as Jeffrey Denberg of the *Atlanta Journal Constitution*, say that Stern isn't concerned enough about the quality of the product, that the commissioner has given in to the owners' demands for easy cash.

However, others, such as Charles Grantham, the executive director of the NBA Players Association, says he admires Stern's leadership on expansion. The owners are clearly looking for the money of expansion, Grantham says, but adds that Stern "is only going to let them expand so much. There's a certain amount you go beyond, it's diminishing returns."

There, between the lines, perhaps, is a partial answer to the NBA's problems. The executive director of the NBA Players Association professes a belief in Stern's leadership, the kind of belief that is echoed across pro basketball, from the media to the players to the owners. The commissioner's business success for the league has brought him a grudging respect. Grantham and the union don't trust him entirely, but they respect his accomplishments. More important, they don't hate him, like the baseball players hate their owners and executives.

Perhaps it's most amazing that in the midst of addressing these worries, Stern still finds time to dream.

Asked about his plans for Mexico, his face brightens. "Well it's got 20 million people or thereabouts," he says. "We've had two exhibition games there, and the enthusiasm has been extraordinary. And the games on television have been well received, and they keep upping the amount.

"I keep thinking in terms of NAFTA and the North American concept. If we've expanded to the 29 million fans to the north (Canada), then there are 80 million more fans south, with Latin America still to come. It seems like a sensible thing to think about."

Asked about language barriers, he responds that the matter is not that simple anymore.

"We're about to live in a different world," he says.

One, you might add, in which the Commissioner is a major player.

CHOKING A BIRD NAMED CHUCK

December 7, 1994 — U.S. Air Arena, Washington, D.C.

From out of the cloud of steam comes Charles Barkley. He's grinning and toting a stack of bath towels, the Phoenix Suns' entire allotment of bath towels. Alas, A.C. Green has noticed this too late and is left stranded, buck naked in the shower without a towel, which is too bad, because the locker room is already filling with reporters, some of them women.

For many NBA players, this would be no problem. After all, they're athletically gifted and proud of it. But Green has deep religious convictions and clearly defined notions about privacy. He sees that famous Barkley grin and knows he's done for. Charles is taking great delight in stranding proud and proper A.C. in his birthday suit.

Green sticks his head out of the shower and stares into a locker room full of amused faces. "Help, Wayman," Green calls to new Suns teammate Wayman Tisdale, himself the son of a preacher. "Help somebody!"

It seems impossible, but Barkley's grin grows even taller. "A.C." he yells as he plunks the stack of towels down near his locker. "It's like Public Enemy says, 'Every brother needs a brother!'"

And every teammate of Charles Barkley needs a remarkably flexible sense of humor. One big enough to work nonstop, around-the-clock. Yet small and transportable. So you can pack it in a suitcase and carry it to every city in the NBA. That's because Charles never stops, never lets up, and even if he does, you can't be certain he's not just setting up the next gag, the next fusillade of blather and grins.

As Utah Jazz president Frank Layden observed a few seasons ago, "Sigmund Freud would jump out of the grave to examine Charles Barkley."

I wouldn't go quite that far, but I would get in the car and drive a few hours as I've done tonight to see Sir Charles take on Chris Webber and the Washington Bullets. Unfortunately, those plans have become derailed, or swamped might be the better word. The employees at the arena here goofed in preparing the ice rink under the basketball floor for an upcoming ice show. The temperature was set too high, leaving a sheen of condensation on the hardwood. Charles knew that it was dangerously slippery the first moment he stepped on it for his early evening warmup. He also knew that arena employees would have no luck in getting it dry in time for the game. Still, they set up large portable fans and mopped and delayed the tipoff two hours in hopes that the conditions would improve. In the interim, both teams relaxed and chatted with each other, turning the on-floor atmosphere into a social gathering. At one point, Barkley even sat on the knee of the Bullets' giant, unassuming center, Kevin Duckworth, who looked a bit surprised and unsure of what to do or say with Charles nonchalantly perched in front of him. Maybe he expected Barkley to whisper his Christmas wish list. Instead, Barkley just sat there, grinning and chatting with the Bullets.

After a while, the arena staff gave up on their efforts to dry the floor and called off the game, which sent the Suns happily scurrying to their locker room, where Barkley found the opportunity to rob A.C. of the towels. Of course, it's purely a power play, something that Charles's teammates have gotten used to, or learned to endure.

"Hey, help!" Green yells again.

"Let's go!" Charles shouts, then turns in mock seriousness to rookie Wesley Person, who is toweling off nearby.

"Let's go," he barks again. "Wes, your ass ain't that f------ dirty. You didn't even play."

Although he's only been in pro basketball a few months now, Person already knows that the best answer for Barkley is a smile. Besides, the hyperactive Sir Charles has already turned his attention away, to begin holding court with the assembly of television cameras, notebooks and microphones that are pinning him against his corner locker. A towel wrapped around his waist, Barkley stretches his long arms between the tops of two corner lockers, like some bald, shiny, Mr. Clean of a crucifix.

Immediately the kleig lights come on and a TV reporter asks him about the game's cancellation. "I was hopin' to play," Barkley deadpans. "I had an injury already picked out. I would have been diving to get hurt. Then I would have been set for life. They could have called me Sonny Liston tonight, because I would have dived all over the place trying to get to the bank."

Apparently sensing that once again the media don't fully realize that he's kidding about filing an accidental injury lawsuit, Barkley shifts to a serious tone. "Really," he says. "Abe Pollin (the Bullets' owner) and the arena people couldn't take chances in that situation. If someone had gotten hurt, they would have been liable."

The game will have to be replayed in April, a radio reporter notes. Could that affect the Suns' playoff drives?

"It doesn't affect a thing," Barkley says. "It just means we'll get to the bar sooner tonight. We should have called it a half hour earlier. I could have had a six pack in my system by now."

It is quite clear that Charles Barkley has the soul of a comic. He'll say absolutely anything that pops into his mind in hopes of getting a laugh. Another reporter smiles and asks who should Barkley point the finger at to blame for the foul up of the floor. "Get a life," Barkley tells him. "You don't go around pointing fingers. What happened tonight was an accident. It was no big deal. Nobody's to blame for it."

That much is true, and the media questions are boring. So I turn to find out what Charles' teammates, who as usual are being ignored by the media, really think of him. I make my way carefully across the crowded room and ask center Joe Kleine, "What's it like to share a locker room with Charles? Does it require a good set of ear plugs?"

He grins. "You ever been in a room full of dirty clothes and it stinks real bad? It's not quite that good."

Standing nearby, guard Dan Majerle begins choking. "Oh, God," he says. "Did I hear that right? Whoa. What's it like to share a locker room with Charles? Have you ever been around a parrot, a macaw, that knows just five or six sayings and says them over and over? The first five or six times you hear it, it sounds pretty funny. But it just keeps saying 'em over and over and over. After a while you just want to f------ strangle the bird?"

"But we love him," adds Kleine, pointing out that the Suns spend many a day listening to a play-by-play from Barkley's Fantasyland. "He's a politician. He's gonna run for governor of Alabama. He's gonna be part owner of a baseball team. He's running this team. He's gonna be on the Senior Tour in golf. There's a little bit of everything in Charles' world.

"And," Kleine confides, "he has these sayings, these Barkleyisms, like, 'Even a blind acorn can find a nut,' or 'Water rises to its own level.' Those are some Barkleyisms. They're all upside down, and nobody's sure what they mean."

Danny Manning has been Barkley's teammate just a few months now, and he's already figured out the secret to survival. The important thing,

Manning says, is not to listen too closely to anything Barkley has to say. And above all, never write it down.

Sir Charles has been in the NBA 11 seasons and the writers covering pro hoops still haven't figured that one out. Barkley just keeps making his outrageous utterances, and they just keep writing 'em down. Like some perpetual game of Simon Says.

As unbearable as all this might seem, his teammates continue to admire Barkley and the media continue to quote him for one simple reason: He is a warrior. An old-fool, old-school warrior. He's a throwback, a 6-4 forward who has excelled by virtue of his strength, his wits and an unequalled desire to put it down right in the faces of a lot of taller men.

"He steps on the court, he wants to win," Manning says. "That's all you can ask of anybody."

Strange as it seems, that's a rare enough commodity in the NBA today. A player who really, really wants to win. Perhaps that's why *GQ* magazine went so far as to include Barkley with that special club of superstars from the 1980s — Magic, Bird and Jordan. They, too, were people who really, really wanted to win. There is, however, one vast difference. The other members all claimed multiple NBA titles for their teams, then retired to other pursuits. Charles, on the other hand, still stalks the pro basketball circuit nightly, like some ghost consigned to a boyish purgatory, in search of that supposedly redemptive jewelry, a championship ring.

Fortunately, Barkley has been able to play out this role in Phoenix, which in recent years has come to be considered the league's choicest locale. He worked his first eight seasons in Philadelphia, having been drafted out of Auburn by the 76ers with the fifth pick in the first round of the 1984 draft. Although Indiana coach Bobby Knight cut him from the 1984 Olympic squad, "the round mound of rebound" (Barkley's first high-profile moniker) made an immediate impact with the 'Sixers and before too long had reduced the City of Brotherly Love to two distinct clubs: those who loved him and those who hated him.

Barkley arrived at the close of Julius Erving's career, and although they had some good teams in their three seasons together, the pair could never lift Philly above the dominant Bird-led Celtics in the Eastern Conference. With Erving's retirement and Boston's demise, the 'Sixers anointed Barkley to return them to another period of greatness. The roster, however, was far too weak for him to mount a legitimate challenge to either the surging Pistons or the Bulls.

Instead, Philadelphia became known for its inconsistent management and ownership, and Barkley's tenure there ended badly. One incident, when he spat at a heckling fan and instead hit a little girl nearby, will dog him to the grave. The matter infuriated Commissioner David Stern, never much of a Barkley fan anyway.

The 'Sixers, though, did have the decency in June 1992 to ship Sir Charles to Phoenix, where things instantly fell in place for him over the 1992-93 season. Like that, he was reborn, earning league MVP honors and leading the Suns to 62 wins and a spot in the championship series against Jordan and his Bulls.

It was a memorable series, not so much for the basketball, but because of the extracurricular activities, which included sightings between games of Barkley and Madonna at a Phoenix restaurant. The championship matchup proved to be Jordan's last go-round, and Barkley was a fitting opponent. It was Charles vs. Michael. Mano y mano. Shaved pate vs. shaved pate. Nike commercial vs. Nike commercial. In his shoe advertisement, Jordan pondered, "What if I were just a basketball player?" while Barkley in his spot declared, "I am not a role model."

That stance only added to the controversy of Sir Charles' public image. Some critics saw him as another highly paid performer shirking his responsibility. Others, though, understood that Barkley's statement was intended as a reminder that pro athletes are merely media images and that the real responsibility for instilling values in young people belongs in the home. Barkley explained as much, but that did little to deter his critics.

As it turned out, both he and Jordan were players, both role models, their determination showing the 1993 NBA Finals' worldwide audience real confidence, real energy. Having come into the league together in the fall of 1984, the two superstars had formed a solid friendship over the years. While Barkley had shown no forethought, no hesitation in trashing his own public image during his early NBA seasons, the more circumspect Jordan had proceeded cautiously, always saying and doing the correct corporate things while persistently building Chicago into a winner. At times, when Barkley's occasional barfights or misguided public statements boiled over into controversy, Jordan had even taken on the task of trying to explain his friend to writers and reporters, the primary message being that Charles may tend to run his mouth before thinking, but he's an honest, genuine person and a tough competitor.

For these defenses and for Jordan's friendship, Barkley was quite grateful. In fact, some said too grateful to be successful in the 1993 championship series. Later, Scottie Pippen, Jordan's teammate, would berate Barkley for "kissin' Michael's ass," an accusation that left Sir

Charles bristling. Yet it would remain one of the great unanswered questions of his career. The Lakers' Magic Johnson and the Pistons' Isiah Thomas had formed a similar friendship in the 1980s, but that relationship fell apart when their teams met in the 1988 and 1989 Finals. There was no way, Johnson later admitted, that their intense competition could not get in the way of their friendship.

Faced with the same tough choice of building and nurturing an intense dislike for his championship competition, Barkley had chosen to remain a good guy and Jordan's friend. The Suns, who had the homecourt advantage in the series, promptly lost the first two games at home in their brand new America West Arena, and the Bulls eventually won 4-2, sending Jordan off to savor his third straight championship in retirement and consigning Barkley to more seasons of dragging his chains around the NBA, looking for what he didn't have.

As if Jordan's abrupt retirement in 1993 hadn't been enough of a disappointment for Barkley, the '93-'94 season produced still more downturns. With Jordan gone from the game, it was supposed to be the year that Barkley finally got his. Instead, Charles was hampered all year by a bulging disk in his back that at times left him looking old. Yet he came alive in the playoffs, scoring 56 points in a first-round game against Golden State, the third highest single-game playoff total in league history. When the Suns took the first two games on the road against favored Houston in the Western semifinals, they seemed set to roll.

In the exuberant aftermath, Barkley was strangely subdued, cautioning his teammates that the series was far from over. What he knew was that the Suns didn't have an answer to Hakeem Olajuwon in the post. Sure enough, Charles' caution proved justified. The Rockets came back to win the series and ultimately to claim the league championship.

Throughout the season, Barkley had suggested that it would be his last. The loss to Houston only confirmed that, with his back aching badly, it was time to call it quits. But he hesitated when the season ended, telling the press he wanted to wait to make his final decision.

Rehabilitating his back would require a rigorous offseason conditioning program, and Barkley, heading toward his 32nd birthday, had never held a fondness for working out. So he spent some time evaluating his impressive list of accomplishments, which included:

- Playing a key role in Dream Team I's gold medal run through the 1992 Olympics
- First team All NBA for five seasons
- A career field goal percentage of .562, second highest among active players
- An eight-time All Star selection
- The 1987 league rebounding title
- League MVP 1993
- All Star Game MVP 1991
- *The Sporting News* Player of the Year in 1991 and 1993 (voted by NBA players)

About the only present not under Barkley's tree was the big one, and if he was careful not to think about it too much, he figured maybe he could walk away.

The Suns were pushing for an answer by the June 29th draft, but Barkley seemed lost in confusion. Fortunately, teammate Danny Ainge was playing with him on the Celebrity Golf Circuit. ("He's terrible," Ainge says of Barkley's golf game.) Ainge spent the month pleading the case for playing another year. "He opened my eyes to a lot of things concerning personal sacrifices," Barkley said. "I want to thank him for staying on my case. 'Persistent' is an understatement. He was riding me hard.

"I was trying to talk myself into retiring. But I wanted somebody to talk me into playing to be honest with you. I wanted to change but I couldn't do it myself."

Ainge simply targeted Sir Charles' substantial pride. "I told him I thought he had a lot of basketball left in him," the veteran guard explained.

Barkley agreed and went to work rehabilitating his back. He arrived in training camp in the best shape in years and felt great during the preseason right up until the moment he suffered a painful stomach injury, a torn muscle.

Instead of playing, he opened the season on injured reserve and watched all his hard-fought conditioning slip away. Ainge was fearful that Barkley might just up and retire rather than try to come back again. That fear grew when he attempted an early comeback and reinjured the muscle.

"Charles came to camp with a real positive attitude and wanted to play," Ainge said. "Then he got hurt and got frustrated. But he stuck with it, and I respect him for that, for living up to the commitment he made this summer, that he's gonna give it everything he's got this year."

The Suns' offseason roster additions also provided Barkley an incentive. Manning had come from Atlanta after agreeing to take a multimillion dollar pay cut just to fit under the Phoenix salary cap. It was an unprecedented move, but Manning thought that he just might be able to provide the extra push to get the title that he and Barkley wanted.

From Sacramento, the Suns got power forward/center Wayman Tisdale. From the draft, they got hot-shooting rookie Person, like Barkley an Auburn alumnus, and from the free-agent market they got rookie point guard Trevor Ruffin.

Although Barkley and point guard Kevin Johnson spent most of the first month of the season on the injured list, this mishmash of new additions and old regulars streaked out to the best record in the Western Conference. Of particular note in this surge was the play of backup point guard Elliot Perry, who filled in nicely for Johnson. All of this warmed the cockles of Barkley's heart, making him all the more eager to return.

Now, it's December, and he's back in the lineup and facing the long prospect of regaining his conditioning. I begin to ask him about that and he abruptly cuts me off. "It happened," he says of the injury. "There's nothing I can do about it. I just hope that I keep getting better. I feel like I am getting better. I felt better during this preseason than I had in a year and a half. Now I just want to get my stomach better and see how good I can play."

Because the Suns have played well so far this year, because they have added several exciting players, many observers have predicted that Phoenix will return to the championship series in 1995. But Barkley remains cautious about his team's prospects. Adding Manning and Tisdale in the offseason meant losing Mark West and Oliver Miller, the Suns' top centers, to Detroit, which left only Kleine and free agent Danny Schayes in the post. Phoenix would have to spend the rest of the season figuring a way to contend with Olajuwon, San Antonio's David Robinson and other quick Western Conference centers.

"We can't tell anything about this team until we get everybody healthy," Barkley says, pointing out that nobody is sure when point guard Kevin Johnson will regain his health.

"We need to get better, we need to get healthy," Ainge agrees.

Just having Barkley back sends them a long way in that direction, although Green and his other teammates have been left to note ruefully that it was Charles' stomach — not his mouth — that had been injured.

Still, they don't mind so much, because despite his image, Barkley is as unfailingly polite as he is mouthy, the result of being raised by his mother and grandmother in the small town of Leeds, Alabama.

In fact, there are Auburn alums in many cities who find their way to the Suns' locker room just to shake Barkley's hand and have a chat.

Now, in the dying moments of a wasted evening, as the locker room is clearing out, one such War Eagle grad approached him. "Thanks a lot for coming by and saying hello," Barkley says, sounding a lot like somebody who wants to be governor.

The Auburn alum makes a quick joke that young Wes Person might someday force a debate as "to who the best player out of Auburn was."

"I don't care who's the best player," Barkley shoots back. "I just want to be the richest one. They can argue over who's best, but I'll be set for life."

Maybe. But only if the Suns play well in June so that he can have that special piece of jewelry that money can't buy.

The team bus is leaving, and an arena employee steps up to tell the few straggling reporters still there that interview time is over.

"It's time, gentlemen," the employee says.

"Don't use that word 'gentlemen' so loosely," Barkley tells him. "After all, these are reporters."

BE LIKE GRANT

DECEMBER 1994

Moving hard to the left of the key, Detroit Pistons point guard Lindsey Hunter bore down on his drive, forcing the wing defender to double team him, which left Grant Hill all alone in three-point land deep in the left corner.

Just like a good point guard is supposed to do, Hunter hit Hill, the Pistons' acclaimed rookie forward, with the pass. Hill considered the shot for an instant, then decided to go for the sure thing. In three lightning steps, he covered the territory down the baseline to the hoop, and with an elongated reach, finished off the move with a simple one-handed stuff.

No rim-rocking. No growl. No thunder.

All the same, his swiftness left the nine other players on the floor standing agape, slack-jawed that he could execute this move before the five defenders could even think about stepping in his way.

"He has an incredible first step," Pistons assistant coach Brendan Malone would say afterward, a phrase repeated often among pro basketball regulars over the first two months of the 1994-95 NBA season.

In fact, Hill so wowed observers in the first weeks of his rookie campaign that he sent them searching for a comparison, and vast numbers of them arrived at the same conclusion: He's like Mike.

Grant Hill's the next Jordan, they said.

THE BEST?

As you might expect, the Jordan comparisons don't sit well with a variety of people, including Hill himself. "I'm flattered," he said. "But the comparisons are crazy."

The NBA, though, has played the name game for years. "It's always premature to compare anybody," says Charles Barkley, "but these media guys have nothing else to do."

"Every time a white guy about 6-9 with a jump shot comes along, he's the next Larry Bird," says Detroit's Malone. "Grant Hill is very good, but he has a lot to learn about the NBA."

It's a classic case of the media overhyping a young player, says Phoenix Suns assistant coach Scotty Robertson, who has nearly a half century of bench experience. "That's a joke," he said. "There's no comparison at this stage. Hill's a rookie. The thing I like about him is the way he's reacted to the members of the press when they've given all these glowing accounts. He says, 'I haven't done anything yet.' And he's right.

"Now he is a great young player. He's the future of that Detroit franchise, like Isiah Thomas once was. But this league will do crazy things to you."

Robertson echoes dozens of people across the league who are cautioning reporters not to link Hill and Jordan. Asked about the comparison, Chicago Bulls general manager Jerry Krause cast a wry, doubtful look and replied, "Michael Jordan's the greatest player in the history of the game. Nobody compares to him."

Yet Billy McKinney, Detroit's director of player personnel, admits that it was actually NBA coaches and scouts — not the media — who first suggested that Hill's moves and instincts reminded them of Michael. The Pistons staff came to this conclusion while watching endless hours of videotape of Hill as a Duke University All-American.

The Pistons took Hill, the son of former Dallas Cowboy running back Calvin Hill, with the third pick of the 1994 draft and signed him to a $45-million contract. Soon after he arrived in Detroit, the rookie made the same favorable impressions with his veteran teammates.

"In my 10 years in the league, he's the best player that I've seen, without a doubt," Detroit guard Joe Dumars said in December. He issued the words slowly, to make sure that the full implication was understood. "Keep in mind that I'm saying this after seeing him play just 14 games."

Dumars, of course, is one of the most respected players in the game. He never makes rash statements. He doesn't traffic in idle talk. This, as you probably know, is the same Joe Dumars who had the unenviable task of guarding Jordan during the classic playoff battles between the Chicago Bulls and the Pistons in 1988, '89, '90 and '91, the rivalry that supposedly challenged Jordan to blossom into a champion.

At the time, Dumars, who was often cited as the league's best defensive guard, spoke with amazement about Jordan's ability to mesmerize a defense, to cause his opponents to freeze in panic and fear. The 22-year-old Hill, Dumars says, has the combination of talent and skills to create that same type of fear in opposing defenses.

But Dumars' appreciation of his new teammate goes far beyond athletics. The same can be said for the league. The NBA's financial growth and expansion has created a wild bidding war for young talent, to the point that polished, veteran players have watched their contracts become eclipsed by the mega-deals signed by rookies fresh out of college. In this year's draft, Purdue's Glenn Robinson held out with the Milwaukee Bucks while his agent sought an unprecedented $100 million contract. Finally exasperated, the Bucks' owner, Wisconsin senator Herb Kohl, suggested that Robinson could take the team and that Kohl would take the fat contract.

Ultimately, Robinson signed a contract in the neighborhood of $60 million, but his case was just one of many that precipitated a building backlash among fans and veteran players against overpriced rookies, some of whom seemed ill-mannered and disrespectful.

Grant Hill, of course, is nothing like that. He is young, bright, polite, respectful — all the good adjectives. Which means that both the NBA and corporate America are eager to promote him.

"Now that I have children, I particularly appreciate Grant Hill," Dumars says. "If I could say that if I wanted my children to be like anyone, that person would be Grant Hill."

THE STAR

As CBS college basketball analyst Billy Packer once pointed out, "Sometimes the public has a sixth sense for greatness." Packer's best example of this is the 1979 NCAA championship game between Indiana State with Larry Bird and Michigan State with Magic Johnson.

Before that spring, both players were relatively unknown on a national level. Yet their meeting in the 1979 championship remains the highest rated Final Four game in history. Quite simply, the fans tuned in because they sensed something very special.

Michael Jordan's arrival in the NBA in 1984 launched a similar phenomenon. Before long, his Chicago Bulls teammates were saying that traveling with the rookie Jordan was like being with a rock star, because of the crowds and fan interest he generated. At the time, the NBA was a backwater pro sport, unused to such attention.

Now, Grant Hill's appearance in a Piston's uniform is setting off another unprecedented response. He has already racked up hundreds of thousands of votes in the fan polling for the 1995 All Star team. His nearest competitor, the ever-present Shaquille O'Neal, lags more than 80,000 votes behind. Never in the history of the game — not Bird, not Magic, not Jordan — has a rookie been the top vote-getter in the All-Star balloting, and old NBA hands are watching to see if Hill can hang on to his lead before the balloting closes in January.

All of which has left the marketing strategists at General Motors smiling broadly. Sensing his impending stardom, the automobile manufacturer had retained him as a spokesman, then cast him in an often-aired television ad in which Hill talks about the pursuit of excellence. In the spot, he quotes his famous father about 90 percent of sports being "from the neck up."

Seldom in the history of sports marketing has a major corporation placed so much faith in an unproven athlete.

In addition, Schick, Wilson, Skybox and Fila, the Italian sportswear manufacturer, have signed him to promotional contracts. Fila announced that it will issue the Grant Hill line of clothing and shoes this spring. It was Nike, of course, who first revolutionized the sportswear business with its wildly successful Air Jordan line.

The only openings left on Hill's plate were a soft-drink manufacturer and a fast-food company, with several competitors hustling to sign him. It seems that the hopes for Hill are as high off the court as on it. The question in the wake of all this is, Why? What's so special about this rookie?

The cynics say there's nothing special about him yet. He's merely a clean, wholesome face with an outstanding pedigree, the perfect pitchman in an age where the emphasis is not on what you've done but what you might possibly do.

Others, however, say that Hill actually brings something fresh to the business. His appeal is a combination of things, says Phoenix Suns guard Danny Ainge. "I love his game. More than anything, though, I love his maturity and how he fits into the team concept. He takes his plays when they come to him. He's very unselfish. Yet he's also very aggressive. He's very confident and very poised. He's gonna be a star."

THE PLAYER

As a freshman and sophomore at Duke, Hill played a key role in the Blue Devils winning back-to-back NCAA championships. As he matured each season, it grew clearer that he was a complete player, documented by the fact that he became the first athlete in Atlantic Coast Conference history to record 1,900 points, 700 rebounds, 400 assists, 200 steals and 100 blocked shots.

At 6-8, he showed unique ballhandling skills. By the time he was a senior, Hill presented one of the truly intimidating figures in the college game. Each time he worked the ball at the top of the key or on the wing, opponents scrambled to arrange their help-side and zone defenses to stop his drives.

In the NBA, Hill presents the same kind of ballhandling intimidation. But in pro basketball, he says, there are no zones and help-side defenses, which means that he has often found a freeway to the hole.

To counter that, defenders have two basic options. They can lay off him and make him take his outside shot, which frankly isn't very strong. Or they can hammer him when he drives in for dunks.

As a pro, Hill has shown a fearlessness about going to the basket. That courage and Hill's hang time on the way to the hoop only fueled the comparisons with Jordan. But Pistons coach Don Chaney said Hill actually reminded him of Rick Barry. "Barry, in his young years, used to go to the basket, get creamed, and then go right back again."

That determination, says Malone, is perhaps Hill's most special asset. "When people start to zero in on him, that's when he shines."

Mostly, defenders began giving him the outside shot, Malone says, and Hill has adjusted by shooting his jumper coming off screens. Or when defenders do stop his drives, he's shown that he can find a teammate with the pass.

His defensive instincts are also special, Malone points out, and that's yet one other reason for the Jordan connection. "Grant can help out by double-teaming in the low post," says the Detroit assistant, "and then recover to the perimeter to still block his man's shot."

THE PERSON

Suns rookie Antonio Lang, who played four years with Hill at Duke, recalled that one day at practice in college, Hill decided he would try to dunk from the foul line. He got a running start at the top of the opposite key, took one dribble, left the ground at the foul line and jammed.

"First time he ever tried to do it," Lang says, shaking his head. "He's quick and he's long. He's very agile. He played soccer a lot when he was young, and I think that has a lot to do with his agility. Plus he has quick moves. He really knows how to extend himself and get to the basket."

It is this athletic ability that has driven the intense public interest in Hill. In every NBA city, dozens of writers and reporters are waiting to interview him. "Everywhere he goes, the electronic and print media want a piece of him," Malone says. "How he handles his celebrity is impressive."

Even though he may be circled by a crowd of reporters, Hill pauses to make eye contact with each questioner, to contemplate the question and deliver a clear answer.

It would be easy for his veteran teammates to grow weary and jealous of the constant attention directed at Hill. But Malone says Hill's low-key manner has meant that the Pistons accept him.

"He's a great guy," Lang says. "He's just as good a guy as he is a basketball player. He believes he's a regular person who's gifted to play basketball."

And Lang doesn't think his former teammate will ever lose that sense of humility. "He has great parents," Lang says. "If he did get out of line, his mother and father would probably kill him. So he realizes that."

Father Calvin is a sports executive, and mother Janet is a lawyer/executive, and their influence is obvious, Lang says. "What he has down pat is that once he's on the court, he can be Grant Hill, the superstar, aggressive and very confident of his game. But once he's off the court, he leaves that kind of person behind."

In fact, Hill is downright human, Lang says. "I've even seen him get busted a few times trying to guard people. He's just like everybody else. But he is talented. With the type of play they have in this league, he's gonna be a megasuperstar."

THE DIFFICULTIES

Yet even Lang cautions about the Jordan comparison. "Mike was in the league a long time and proved himself a long time," Lang says. "I think Grant has the ability to be that type player, but it's going to take some time. Before people can compare him to Jordan, he's gonna have to stick in there like Mike."

He's certainly going to have to make the same uphill climb. Jordan came to a Bulls' roster riddled with cocaine abusers in 1984. He disdained the party life and averaged 28 points while trying to help a bad team become better.

Hill, too, is faced with trying to lift the fortunes of a struggling club. The Pistons, though, have been plagued by injuries, not drugs. Averaging 19 points, Hill led them to a surprising start the first month of the season, but Detroit's fortunes soon plummeted as point guard Hunter and centers Mark West and Oliver Miller were felled by injuries.

Hill himself was slowed by nagging foot injuries and acknowledged that the pace of the pro schedule and the travel required left him exhausted. One of his goals in the offseason surely will be to add muscle to his angular frame.

Even so, he has been what many consider to be the NBA's most intriguing rookie in years. Even Hill himself has quietly admitted that while he has yet to accomplish anything as a professional, his goal is to become "the greatest player in the history of the game."

He knows he's a long way from even getting close to that.

The question is, are Hill and other young superstars good enough to present a challenge that might lure Jordan out of retirement?

After all, Hill won two NCAA titles at Duke, and Jordan won only one at North Carolina. Hill is already ahead in the jewelry count.

Lang laughs at the idea of Hill challenging Jordan. "I hope Mike stays out of the league!" he says. One other thing, he adds with a cackle. "Don't tell Grant he's like Jordan. He doesn't need to think he's that good."

HIGHWAY TO HELL
DECEMBER, 1994

For Jack Haley, the wild ride began innocently enough. He was merely assigned a locker next to Dennis Rodman in the San Antonio Spurs dressing room. At the time, it didn't seem like such a big deal. After all, Haley's affiliation with the Spurs held little potential for a long-term relationship. It was December 1993, and he had just been claimed off the waiver wire, the latest stop in a herky-jerky pro career that had seen him play for six different teams in seven seasons.

Haley, however, wasn't complaining. He was lucky to even be there. Not many players who average a mere 3.7 points and 4.4 rebounds per game in college manage to make it in the NBA. Yet that's just what Haley had done after playing three unimpressive seasons at UCLA. In fact, he hadn't even participated in high school basketball. He had grown up on Southern California's beaches, the son of the 1959 U.S. Surfing champion. Young Haley might have followed the old man, but his adolescent pituitary proved to be a complicating factor; it worked overtime, pushing him way up there to 6-foot-10, far too tall for a surfer dude. So he left behind the world of waves and entered into the realm of hoops. His first stop on the basketball circuit was some playing time at little Golden West College, and that in turn opened up the opportunity to play at UCLA, where he met Stacy, a perfectly blonde embodiment of the California girl. She was a Bruin cheerleader who would become his wife, just one of many fancy turns in the charmed life of Jack Haley.

Figuring him for a project, the Bulls selected Haley in the fourth round of the 1987 draft because he had size and could play a little position defense. Plus he was white, and that was usually good enough for a late round pick in the old days of the NBA's expanded draft.

Failing to catch on immediately in Chicago, Haley played his first pro season in the Spanish league and averaged a surprising 20.2 points and 10.3 rebounds per game, good enough for the Bulls to sign him for the 1988-89 season. He played in 51 games and averaged 2.2 points, but early in the '89-90 campaign Chicago let him go. Fortunately the New Jersey Nets pulled him off the waiver wire, and he held on there for nearly two seasons. In fact, he played better than 1,100 minutes in 1990-91 and averaged a career-high 5.6 points per game, all of which prompted the Lakers to sign him as a free agent. He played one active season in Los Angeles and spent yet another on injured reserve.

Then, in November 1993, the Lakers introduced him to the waiver wire yet again, which was how he had landed in San Antonio. If nothing else, his survival had shown Haley to be quite adept at filling the role of 12th or 13th man on an NBA team. Raised among Hollywood's entertainment elite, Haley had learned early enough that his smile and good looks could take him a long ways (his sister, Sonya, had worked as an assistant press secretary for George Bush and would later catch on as Director of Corporate Communications for the NBA). In the offseason, he dabbled in show business and had even made an appearance in Aerosmith's video "Love in an Elevator." His real claim to fame, however, was his absolute mediocrity as an NBA role player. He knew how to cheer from the bench, knew how to be supportive of his teammates, knew how to work in practice, and knew how enjoy a ride or two on the 'injured reserve' list, all of which were essential skills for anyone who hoped to collect the NBA's minimum $250,000 annual salary as a deep sub.

After six years in pro basketball, Jack Haley knew that to make it with a team he had to establish relationships as quickly as he established his game. Sure, Rodman's troubled reputation preceded him, but Haley figured he could hit it off with anyone, even a sullen, tattooed man with dyed hair and earrings.

"I walked in," Haley recalled of that first day, "and said, 'Hey, howyadoin? I'm Jack Haley.' He wouldn't even acknowledge I was in the room or shake my hand. We sat next to each other for almost three months and never spoke a word. I would try occasionally. I'd say, 'Hey, howyadoin?' I'd get no response. Just like the rest of the team."

To all of the Spurs, Rodman posed a giant mystery, and he seemed a bit wounded.

Like everyone else in the NBA, Haley had heard the rumors about Rodman from his days with the Pistons. First the mercurial forward had been upset that the Detroit organization drove away Chuck Daly, the coach that Rodman worshipped as a father figure. Then the team, once loud, proud league champions, began to slip noticeably over the 1992-93 season with former assistant Ron Rothstein as head coach. All in all, it was a troubled year for Rodman. He missed 17 games with a torn calf muscle, but worse, he openly challenged the new Pistons regime and was twice suspended for violations of team rules. Many of his troubles developed when Rodman learned that the longtime girlfriend whom he had recently married had developed a relationship with one of his best friends, a former teammate. His subsequent divorce forced a traumatic turn of events in which a despondent Rodman reportedly threatened suicide, leading to press reports questioning his mental stability.

Although some people in the Pistons organization had long worried that Rodman was fundamentally troubled, many in Detroit simply saw him as a fun-loving, immature guy who could be surprisingly sweet. One of his favorite pastimes was hanging out with teenagers in mall game rooms (growing up in Dallas he had gotten the nickname 'Worm' from his nastiness playing pinball.) He was also known for handing out big bills to the city's many street people, and one time he reportedly took a homeless man to his house, fed him, gave him a bath and handed the wide-eyed fellow $500.

This 'giving' side was just more proof that Rodman was hardly the typical NBA player, the kind of actions that prompted former Piston teammate John Salley to say that Dennis Rodman was one of the few "real people" in the NBA. Certainly he was unlike many other NBA players in that he had not come up through the ranks of the great American basketball machine, he had not been on scholarship his entire life, wearing the best shoes and equipment and staying in fancy hotels where the meal checks were always paid. Rodman had missed all of that.

The first child of Philander and Shirley Rodman, Dennis spent the early years of his life in New Jersey where his father served in the Air Force. Philander Rodman showed a propensity for living up to his name, so much so that finally Shirley Rodman grew tired of strange women calling the house. When Dennis was three, she packed up her family and moved it back to her native Dallas. It was there that Dennis spent his formative years, a wormy little momma's boy who spent long hours pining for his father, which proved to be a debilitating factor throughout his childhood and adolescence.

His two younger sisters, Debra and Kim, would become high school basketball stars and later college basketball All-Americans, but Dennis had no such luck. If his adolescence had a context, it was a shyness framed by fear and insecurity. To make matters worse, his younger sisters both grew taller than he was, leaving Dennis behind as a frail runt, the kind of guy who had to fear for his lunch money at school each day.

In tenth grade at South Oak Cliff High School, he tried out for the football team and didn't make the cut. Although he was only 5-9, basketball was a little better. He at least made the team but quit midway through the season because he never got to play. Next he tried the bass viola for a time but gave up on that, too. Like many teen boys, his self esteem was the size of his pinkie, which meant that "hangin' out" became his activity of choice. In game and pool rooms. Fastfood parking lots. Rec centers. Anywhere a few driftless hours could be killed. It was a world that reflected his career aspirations. While his mom was an English teacher and his sisters were on the fast track, Dennis' future prospects were limited. He figured he might be able to finish high school, get a job and maybe buy a car.

Until that day happened, his one salvation was his mom's Monte Carlo, his ticket to joyrides and relationships with guys in the neighborhood. The car even provided a reason for his part-time jobs: All he wanted was a little money for gas and maybe snazzy hubcaps and foglights. Like millions of other American kids, he floated in this netherworld. He endured tongue lashings from his mother for snitching $5 bills from her purse for entertainment funds, and spent long, lonely hours cruising around. He saw very little purpose in life and didn't seem particularly troubled about his prospects.

He got a job as a valet at a local car dealership but was soon fired for taking a joy ride. He did manage to graduate from high school, yet his lack of success seemed all the more pronounced when compared with his sisters' accomplishments. Both were high school hoops stars on their way to celebrated college careers. At 6-2, Debra would play for Louisiana Tech, and 6-foot Kim went on to excel at Stephen F. Austin.

Dennis, meanwhile, was headed nowhere, cast into a sea of slack after high school, a series of menial day jobs and a part-time night gig mopping and sweeping up at Dallas-Fort Worth Airport. It was there, on the dare of a coworker, that he stuck a broom handle through an airport gift shop grate and stole 15 watches, which he later passed out to friends.

Within days, he was arrested and jailed, only to confess under grilling by detectives. The charges were dropped after Rodman gave police details on how to recover the property, but not before he spent a night in jail, during which, Rodman later admitted, he was "scared s---less."

Even this setback and the loss of his job couldn't budge him into change. Ultimately, Rodman's life would be rescued by his pituitary. He grew 11 inches in one amazing year, yet even that only increased his isolation. By age 20, he was 6-8 and had outgrown his clothes, leaving his only attire the oversized coveralls from his job washing cars. About the only place he didn't feel like a geek was the playgrounds. Pickup basketball had become his refuge, and his height was one of his first real advantages in life.

It was one of his sisters' friends who got him a tryout at Cooke County Junior College in nearby Gainesville, Texas. He figured there was little hope, but the coaches jumped at the opportunity to sign an athletic big man and gave him a two-year ride right on the spot.

He became an immediate starter at center at Cooke and averaged double figures in rebounds despite the fact that he was playing organized ball for the first time in his life. It didn't matter. College seemed so strange. He dropped out after a few months but not before catching the eye of Lonn Reisman, an assistant coach at Southeastern Oklahoma State.

Back home in Dallas, Rodman soon found himself adrift, tossed out of the house by his mother. It was Reisman who came to his rescue with yet another scholarship offer. Southeastern was in the tiny farming community of Bokchito, Oklahoma, several hours north of Dallas. Rodman was very skeptical of going, but then again, he had few choices.

One of his first tasks there was serving as a counselor for the school's summer basketball camp. Within days of his arrival, Rodman befriended 13-year-old Bryne Rich, a white camper from a nearby farm. The previous Halloween, Rich had accidentally shot and killed his best friend while quail hunting. The ensuing months had left him almost paralyzed by depression, so much so that his parents feared for his future. Then one day the next summer, Bryne came home from camp all enthused about the new counselor he had met, "The Worm," Southeastern's new basketball recruit.

Fraternization between the races wasn't exactly common in Bokchito, population 607, but Bryne Rich's parents were willing to go along with anything that rescued their son from the aftermath of the hunting accident. Bryne and Dennis formed an almost instant brotherly attachment and were well on their way to helping each other out of the shadows. Within days, Rodman was invited to dinner. Once there, he was invited to sleep over for the night, and he wound up staying three years with the Rich family, an experience detailed in the book *Rebound, The Dennis Rodman Story*, authored by Rodman, writer Alan Steinberg and Pat Rich, Bryne's mother.

On the court, Rodman became something of a force in NAIA basketball, averaging nearly 26 points and 16 rebounds over the next three seasons.

He led the Southeastern Oklahoma State Savages to a district title and into contention for the NAIA national title (with young Bryne serving as an assistant manager for the team).

That performance, in turn, led to the Pistons selecting Dennis with the 27th pick in the 1986 draft, which marked the next giant step in the amazing turnaround in Rodman's life. As a rookie, Rodman found himself thrust into the titanic playoff struggle between Detroit and Larry Bird's Boston Celtics, who after winning three championships over the previous six seasons, had started their trek into decline. The Celtics, however, managed to survive one last hard-fought, emotional battle with the Pistons in the 1987 playoffs. Rodman's defense on Bird had caught the eye of keen NBA observers, and the rookie caught the rest of the basketball world's attention when he opined afterward that if he weren't white, Bird would be just another good basketball player.

Of course, the predominantly white media and pro hoops fan base treated Bird like an icon, but they were outraged at having a Pistons' rookie call their hand at it. To make matters worse, Pistons captain Isiah Thomas had agreed with Rodman, and the ensuing outcry had left Thomas trying to explain away his opinions. Eventually, both sides came to an understanding that Bird was one of the greatest players of all time, but there was little question that his appreciation by the fans and the media was much more intense because of his race.

For Rodman, this iconoclastic beginning was just the first of many notices he would send. Before long, the coaches, players, fans and media involved with the NBA would get the message: He was far from the average player. In fact, the defense and rebounding of the shy young forward were key factors in the Pistons defeating the Celtics in 1988 and rising to league championship contention. I covered the team during those years and remember talking to Rodman in the locker room just moments after the Pistons defeated the Lakers for the 1989 NBA title.

Strangely enough, we talked about pinball and the natural hyperactivity that fed his hoops nastiness. "My friends knew I was hyper. Real hyper," he said of his days growing up in Dallas. "They knew I wouldn't settle down, I wouldn't sleep. I'd just keep going.

"And now I just focus my energy in something I love to do. Now, I just play basketball, go out there and have a lot of fun and enjoy."

The joy was obvious in his gait, which itself seemed almost out of character with "The Worm." In warmups, he would run erect, proudly, springing off each toe, then kicking his heels up behind him almost daintily. There was something almost Victorian in his posture as he jogged, something old-fashioned, something prim, smacking of Casey at the Bat and barbershop quartets, or some other cockiness from a long-lost era. Rodman, in that way, was a throwback. . . until you saw him fill the lane on a fastbreak when he threw off all the pretensions. Then, he was just a blur. There would be Isiah Thomas, running the show from the center of the floor, with Rodman to the right. Thomas would encounter a defender and toss a fat lob up for Rodman, who would be curling from the right and rising high, almost higher it seemed than the glass. The ensuing slam would be executed with an impressive enthusiasm. Rodman would land with a jet skid, a tight angle, fall back a bit, catch himself with his left hand and right himself with rocketlike quickness, rising straight up in the air for the crowd, jutting the index finger. He was number one, or somebody was number one. Anyway, before you could blink, the hyperactivity had refilled his tanks as he circled and headed back upcourt where he could have some real fun and play defense, making somebody's night very miserable.

At these times, it occurred to me that Dennis Rodman was the past and the present all rolled into one.

After a time, it became clear that there was not one pure basketball fan in America, not even one with the greenest of Celtic hearts, who didn't absolutely love the way he played, with that very tangible desire.

Back in the netherworld of Dallas, he had worked briefly pounding fenders in an auto body shop. You could still see some of that in his game. But like any smart player with unrefined offensive skills, Rodman made his living on the offensive boards. When the Pistons had the ball, he would often back away from the lane, his hands on his hips, his eyes always on the guards working the ball on the perimeter. He watched intently, waiting to make his move, waiting to get that special little piece of position for an offensive rebound. That was his primary study, his soul's joy of joys. Sometimes, after he had snuck in and stolen an offensive rebound, he would dribble out to the perimeter, stand there with the ball in one palm and punch the air with his other fist. He would usually do this in the Palace of Auburn Hills, the Pistons' fancy arena, where the crowds would bathe him in warm applause, and he would stand there, soaking in the ineffable glow of limelight.

After watching him in the 1989 Finals, Chick Hearn, the great Laker broadcaster, declared that Rodman was the best rebounder in the game. That night, after the championship, I told him of Hearn's assessment. Rodman was stunned. "The best rebounder?" he asked, his eyes blinking in the first light of understanding. "In the game? You mean they put me in front of Oakley, Barkley, all those guys? I wouldn't say that. I think I'm one of the best ones, one of the top 10. But I can't be the best rebounder. I'm just in a situation where they need my rebounding here. I rebound with the best of them even though I'm not as bulky as some guys. I use my ability to jump and my quickness to get around guys."

It was Chuck Daly who had persuaded him to use these advantages to become a superb rebounding specialist and defender. Rodman bought into the plan and worked to make himself a marvelously versatile sub. Quick enough to stay with Michael Jordan or any other big guard/small forward in the league. Motivated enough to play power forward. Even tough enough to survive at center against much bigger bodies.

At Daly's suggestion, he had made this approach his mission after the 1987 Playoffs. "I just came to training camp and said, 'Hey, I want to play defense,'" Rodman recalled. "Then the 1988 playoffs really got me going. I just told myself, 'It's time to start focusing on something you really want to do.' I just feel like defense is something I really want to do."

This, of course, was almost a strange approach for pro players, the vast majority of which are unduly preoccupied with their scoring averages and care not a whit about playing sweaty, smelly defense. Rodman, however, described his approach as "focusing in on the guys that I have to play and bearing down on what I need to do to stop this guy. Just having the hunger and desire to want to do the job. Because not many guys in this league want to play defense. Not many guys want to do that. If you can kind of put it in your mind and say, 'Hey, I know I got to play defense because I know I'm not going to score as much; I know I'm not going to get the ball on offense.' So why would I exert myself on offense when I can exert myself on defense?"

Daly, of course, couldn't have been more pleased if he had asked the question himself. Rodman moved into the starting lineup for 1989-90 and helped the Pistons to yet another championship. From there, however, Detroit's guard-oriented offense declined. The Pistons were swept by Chicago in the 1991 playoffs, and although they made a playoff run in 1992, Daly moved on to coach the New Jersey Nets, leaving Dennis without the fatherly coaching connection he badly wanted. When his off-court problems were added to the mix, it became time for his tenure in Detroit to end.

That October of 1993, the Pistons traded Rodman to the Spurs for forwards Sean Elliot, David Wood and "future draft considerations," thus igniting the next amazing stage in the transformation of Dennis Rodman.

From all accounts, he came to San Antonio a changed man. As Rodman explains it, "I woke up one day and said to myself, 'Hey, my life has been a big cycle. One month I'm bleeding to death, one month I'm in a psycho zone.' Then all of a sudden the cycles were in balance."

He had decided to say, "F--- it," which left him searching through a series of tattoo shops, piercing pagodas, alternative bars and hair salons to find the real Dennis. Above all, Rodman knew one thing. He would be very careful about who he trusted, particularly when it came to teammates.

"I mean, c'mon," Haley said. "The guy gets married. He's been married for 80 days. He finds out his best friend in the world is sleeping with his wife. Wouldn't you be a little depressed? Wouldn't that make you a little bummed out? To get a divorce after 80 days. The mother of your daughter who means everything to you. Your best friend. And you lost both of them? Your team is losing, too? That would throw a downslide on my day. My reaction would have been to kill them, not myself."

FAST FRIENDS

Jack Haley watched in amazement that winter of 1994 as Rodman moved in and silently took control of the power forward spot in San Antonio, giving David Robinson the kind of help that he'd never enjoyed before. Soon Rodman was regularly pulling down 20 rebounds a game, an astounding feat.

"I'm a rebounder by trade," Haley said, "and I figured they were padding his stats. I figured no one could get 20 rebounds a night. So I started counting his rebounds. I'd come to him in a game and say, 'You got 17. You need three more.' Or, 'You need two more.' Or, 'You're having an off night. You only got five.' One game, he said to me, 'How many rebounds do I have?' From there, we developed a slow dialogue."

Perhaps it was the fact that Haley is one of the least threatening people in the NBA. Perhaps, it was the fact that he was patient, that he made a low-key effort. Whatever it was, this casual acceptance somehow accelerated into a full-blown friendship about midway through the season.

"It really shocked me," Haley said. "We were at our team black tie dinner. Dennis and I had talked a couple of times. After the dinner was over, I'm standing there with my wife. I'm in a tuxedo. He pulls up in his Ferrari, and he says, 'Hey, would you and your wife like to go to dinner with me and my girlfriend?' We say, 'Sure.' And we went to a restaurant and had a nice dinner, and he said, 'Do you guys want to go to a bar?'

I said, 'Yeah, we'll go to a bar.' He takes my wife and I to a club, and it says right on the door, 'San Antonio's number one gay and alternative nightclub.' I think he was just trying to shock me to see what kind of guy I was. So we went in, and they had a male stripper up on the stage, stripped down to a G-string. I shocked him and slipped one of the guys a buck. Ever since then, we've been good buds. I let him know, 'Hey, this is not my world, but I'm not shocked by it.'"

Indeed, Haley found he could hang rather easily on Rodman's zany planet, among his offbeat circle of friends, including a growing number of celebrities, models, hairdressers, gamblers, coin dealers and whoever else happened to nudge in beside Rodman at the craps tables of life. Almost overnight, the pair became inseparable, tooling around in Rodman's pink-and-white custom Ford monster truck, watching television at Rodman's house amid the clatter of his 15 exotic birds and two German shepherds, jetting back and forth to Vegas and L.A., carousing all night, tossing back shots of Jaggermeister and Goldschlager... Instead of a sullen, depressed guy, Haley discovered a Rodman who was ebullient, a personality bubbling from a ceaseless energy further hypercharged by nibbling chocolate-covered coffee beans. "If you're within the elite circle, he is the life of the party," Haley says. "You can't shut him up. He's hilarious. A great guy to be around."

Conversely, Rodman found Haley to be wonderfully accommodating, like a big puppy eager to please. If nothing else, Haley's Southern California background, his rock video experience, his Hollywood connections, his innate sense of cool, had intrigued Rodman. Plus, on the Spurs' roster of holy rollers, Rodman saw Haley as a relief. At least he wasn't always preaching the Gospel.

Still, to observers, they seemed like an odd couple. Here was Jack Haley. Nice guy. Clean cut. All-American. And there was Dennis Rodman. Obviously on the highway to hell. And honking his horn to get into a passing lane.

Before long, though, their relationship became apparent to those around them. Haley and Rodman had the simplest yet strongest of bonds. They needed each other.

Haley needed Rodman to legitimize his NBA existence, and Rodman needed Haley to interpret his actions and communicate his feelings and intentions to the people he didn't want to deal with, mostly the players and management of the San Antonio Spurs.

After all, somebody had to keep at least one foot in the real world. At first, Spurs officials snidely remarked that Haley was clinging to Rodman to keep a job in the NBA. Later, though, when Haley was trying to hold the team together in the midst of several Rodman storms, team officials had completely changed that evaluation. "Jack has been huge," one Spurs official confided.

TUMBLING DICE

Most relationships have a dark side, and for Dennis Rodman and Jack Haley, it was their shared passion for gambling. For Haley, it was baccharat. For Rodman, it was rolling bones. During the season, they would catch a quick plane to Vegas whenever the opportunity arose. In the summers, they flew there nearly every weekend, making as many as 19 trips in one summer, always staying at the Mirage, where, Haley says, "they treat us like royalty."

For years, Chuck Daly had worried that Rodman was going through all of his money, that he was throwing it away on the craps tables in Vegas. Time would show that those fears were well-founded.

"Dennis is not a shy gambler," Haley said. "He plays for very big stakes. That's one of the things we have in common. I'm a big gambler myself. We spend a lot of time in Vegas. We're out there a large portion of the summer. We fly in and out. I mean Las Vegas is a big part of our lives. Dennis plays nothing but craps. I'm a bachharat player. Of course, we'll play each other's. I'll play craps with him, and he'll play bachharat with me. If we play say eight hours a day, he'll be on the crap table seven and a half hours."

On the bad nights, Rodman has lost as much as $30,000. At times, though, things have gotten worse. Much worse.

Haley says, "The biggest night I've ever seen Dennis have, I think he won $89,000 one night. I've seen him drop $200,000 in a weekend. Part of the $200,000 he lost, though, was the $89,000 he had won the week before. He won 89 the trip before, and we went back, and instead of the average $500 bet, it was a $5,000 bet. The next thing you know you're in big trouble. (Haley later said in a subsequent interview that he misspoke here. Given time to reflect on his earlier comments, he said that he actually never saw Rodman lose the $200,000 but only heard about it later. "The most I saw him lose in one night was about $30,000," Haley said.)

"One thing that impressed me more than anything, he was losing and he was losing huge. We pulled up at the airport to get out of the taxi, and the cab was only six bucks, and he said, 'I got it.'"

Rodman just didn't seem to know when it was time to let somebody else pick up the tab, just as he didn't know when it was time to quit.

"Later we went right back at them and recouped a portion of the losses," Haley said. "This was during the summer. During the season, you're in and out. You can't lose that much money. You set a limit for yourself every night."

Isn't the league concerned about the gambling? I asked Haley during an interview.

"What can the league say to him?" he replied. "What can they say? That's legalized gambling. They can't tell us how much money to bet. We're not Michael Jordan. We're not betting a million dollars, but we're betting more than the average player. People have to put it in perspective. If a regular person goes, and they lose a thousand dollars in Las Vegas, what's the difference if a guy making $2.5 million loses $10- or $20,000? It's the same thing."

A MATERIAL GUY

Yes, he was a great defender and rebounder. Yes, he had the dyed hair and tattoos and earrings. But the strange and wacky ways of Dennis Rodman wouldn't have interested us nearly so much if he hadn't been home one night with Haley watching a Knicks game on cable.

"Dennis and I are watching a Knicks game on TV," Haley said. "Madonna is in Madison Square Garden and they interview her after the game, talking about NBA players. She makes a comment to the effect that of all the players in the league she thinks the sexiest guy is Dennis Rodman. Of course we pounce on that.

"We decided to let our PR guy contact her PR person. And her person actually said, 'Yes, Madonna is writing an article for *Vibe* magazine.' So they got back to us, and Madonna said, 'Can I interview you?' Dennis said, 'Sure.' Dennis hops on a plane after a game, flies to Miami to meet with Madonna for this supposed interview. They did a five-minute token interview, then went out on the town, danced all night and had a great time, spent the night together. From there, it was phone calls, faxes, conversations everyday."

"She had ways of making you feel like King Tut," Rodman says wistfully. "But she also wanted to cuddle and be held."

"They got along very well," Haley says. "Madonna and Dennis saw each other several times. Then we went to Los Angeles. She has a home there, and that was the first time I actually met her and went out with her. I was very impressed with Madonna as a lady. I was kind of shocked. Her image as a hard cutthroat lady with profanity, she was nothing like that. She was polite, and in a partying sense, too. It was not just, 'Oh, hi, how ya' doin'?' She was well-spoken and outstanding. But you can feel her power and presence when you're with her. She wants it her way or no way. She's accustomed to that, and Dennis is the same way, so there was some conflict there.

"They had only been dating a month or so, and she starts talking to Dennis about having a baby. She's definitely interested in having a baby. She says to me, 'Jack, I want Dennis to have my baby.' I said, 'Why, Madonna, would you want Dennis Rodman to have your baby?' She said, 'Dennis Rodman is the perfect physical specimen to have my child.' I said, 'Well, did you ever consider the mental side?' They all laughed when I said that. That was her only response."

Rodman obviously loved the warmth of Madonna's caresses, but the heat of her bright white media was an even bigger turn-on, which isn't too surprising. Just about everybody gets lathered up in the presence of her celebrity. Even Spurs coach John Lucas got his head and perhaps his priorities turned around that spring of 1994. Actually, there was mounting concern about Lucas' laissez faire approach with Rodman even before Madonna happened on the scene. The coach was obviously happy to have the rebounding/defending forward on the team, and he decided the best way to keep Rodman happy and motivated was to allow him to live by a different set of rules than the rest of the Spurs, which is to say almost no rules at all.

"He gave Dennis way too much leeway," Haley would later say of Lucas. "Dennis did not have to come to practice if he didn't want to. Dennis did not have to ride the team bus if he didn't want to. Dennis would not have to come to a game until 20 or 30 minutes before tipoff. And that causes team dissension. How can a guy walk in 15 minutes before the buzzer and still start? And have the coach basically say, 'So what?'"

Perhaps it's unfair to say that Madonna's presence was a distraction to the Spurs over the spring of 1994 as they closed in on a 55-win season. But April was the first month during the entire campaign in which the club posted a losing record, four wins and seven losses. As the regular season edged to a close, Rodman was assured of claiming his third straight league rebounding title with a 17.3 average. David Robinson, however, was in a neck-and-neck race with Orlando Magic center Shaquille O'Neal for the league scoring title, with both hovering just above 29 points per game.

The Spurs faced the hapless Los Angeles Clippers at the L.A. Sports Arena on the last day of the regular season. To make sure Robinson won the title, Lucas turned his center loose. Robinson scored 71 points to boost his average to 29.8 beyond O'Neal's 29.3, and the Spurs won, 112-97. In the excitement of the aftermath, Lucas turned to Madonna, who was sitting courtside, grabbed her hand and led her into his team's locker room.

"Lucas grabs her hand, walks her into the locker room for our postgame meeting," Haley says. "She then stays in the locker room for the duration, as all 12 players shower and change, saying there's nothing she hasn't seen before."

Several media accounts of the game would report that it was Rodman who had taken Madonna into the locker room. But Rodman himself was just as shocked as the rest of the players to turn around and find his famous girlfriend with that come-hither smile amidst the steam and sweat of the Spurs' postgame meeting.

The Spurs were then scheduled to host the Utah Jazz in a first-round, best-of-five playoff series. The Spurs won handily in the first game in San Antonio, but in the second game they went scoreless for 16 minutes and watched the Jazz control the outcome. Even worse, Rodman clobbered Utah guard John Stockton and was suspended for the critical Game 3 in Salt Lake City. Despite the suspension, Madonna showed up in Utah with Rodman.

"At this point, they were probably at their peak," Haley said. "Love is flying in the air, and everything's great. But Dennis was suspended for one game. He, of course, took off with Madonna, left Salt Lake City and went up to Park City, Utah, to one of those love resorts where they have the heart-shaped jacuzzis and the whole thing. They hid up there from the press, because there was a media frenzy. No one, management or coaching staff, knew Dennis' whereabouts but me, and I had to relay in between.

"I was eating it up, though," Haley said with a laugh. "I was on TV doing Madonna and Dennis updates for four days. It was great. And they were doing great."

The Spurs, however, were headed down in an upset with two losses in Utah. "We get knocked out of the playoffs," Haley said. "Dennis has 22 or 23 rebounds. He plays great, but we lose the game. Dennis walks off the floor, directly into the locker room, picks up his gym bag with his clothes, walks right out of the locker room, still in his Spurs uniform, saying nothing to anyone but me, does not wait for the post game comments from John Lucas or anyone. He and Madonna get directly into a limousine, drive out of the arena while all of these people are screaming, drives straight to the airport, hops on a private plane and goes straight to Las Vegas, where they have a great time."

In the aftermath of the Spurs' loss, Rodman's suspension and his apparent callousness about team issues created a storm of media criticism, much of it directed at his removing his shoes while on the bench during a game. Lucas and Spurs general manager Bob Bass were shown the door. Even Rodman's affair with Madonna seemed to suffer. After all, he still had a live-in girlfriend in San Antonio.

"Madonna finds out," Haley said, "and a couple of weeks later Dennis is in Vegas with this other girl. Madonna comes to Vegas, checks into the suite right next to him."

Rodman later told Haley that Madonna accosted him and suggested, "Let's hit a little white chapel right now and get married."

Haley added, "Dennis says, 'No.' But he leaves his girlfriend in Las Vegas, doesn't tell her where he's going. He says he's going to work out. Instead, he hops on a plane and flies back to Los Angeles with Madonna and hides out."

Meanwhile, his poor Texas girlfriend is stuck in Vegas wondering what happened to Rodman, Haley said. "It took her two days before she realized Dennis wasn't coming back. He's known to hang out and be flighty anyway, so the girlfriend ends up calling me in L.A. I'm there with Dennis and Madonna, and she's asking me where Dennis is. I finally have to tell her, 'You should go on home.' I sent her a plane ticket to get home."

It seemed like a hard-hearted way to break up with somebody, but Rodman had bigger things on his mind. Madonna was still pressing him to get married. "I told him, 'Don't do it,'" Haley later admitted. "Huge error on my part. I admit it now. I said, 'Don't do it.' Bad mistake now in hindsight. The settlement would have been huge. He could have still been getting alimony."

Lord knows he needed the money.

YOU'RE IN THE ARMY NOW

To replace Bob Bass as general manager in May 1994, the Spurs hired Gregg Popovich, who had once been an assistant coach in San Antonio. The most important factor, however, was that he came from a military background and ran the team from that experience. He had played college ball at the Air Force Academy in the late 1960s, then went on to a five-year military commitment during which he played service ball on an Armed Forces team that won the 1971 AAU title. Once his military playing days were over, Popovich returned to the Air Force Academy as an assistant coach for six years, then moved on to the University of Denver before spending nearly a decade as head coach of Pomona-Pitzer College in California. His academy background helped Popovich jump to Larry

Brown's Spurs staff as an assistant coach in 1988, just as David Robinson was preparing to leave the Navy and enter the NBA.

Popovich spent four seasons in San Antonio, then moved on to an assistant's job with the Golden State Warriors for two seasons. That, in turn, led to his hiring as the Spurs' general manager.

From the loosely run organization they had been, the Spurs underwent dramatic change over the summer of 1994. With his military background, Popovich reorganized the Spurs, which maybe explains their choice of armed guards for their 1994 training camp in the Texas Hill Country.

The transition was not an easy one for Dennis Rodman. "That set up a huge problem," Haley explained. "How, as a player, do you go from getting away (with almost anything) to almost a militaryesque coaching staff?"

Despite his childhood rejection by a father who served in the military, Rodman's real problem with the Spurs wasn't their new dress-formation approach. It was purely money.

"Dennis came to San Antonio under John Lucas and Bob Bass, and he was promised a $6-million bonus if he played well that year," Haley said. "He went on to grab his third rebounding title and played well, and the team did well and lost in the first round of the playoffs. Dennis' being suspended that one game definitely was a contributing factor, but Dave had a very rough playoff against the Jazz. But our whole team at that time just wasn't ready to compete. So we lost. The Spurs then asked Bob Bass to retire, and John Lucas moved to Philadelphia. And they hired Gregg Popovich and Bob Hill."

Rodman immediately wanted the money he had been promised by Bass, but Popovich declined.

"Dennis felt, here he is a three-time rebounding champion, a guy who is well-proven," Haley said. "He's looking around the league. Grant Hill comes in and is given $5- or $6-million a year. Rookie after rookie is making more money than Dennis is. J.R. Reid, who plays behind Dennis, is making more money than he is. Terry Cummings makes more money. Dennis says, 'Hey, what about me? You promised me this money. I was expecting it. What's happened?' They came to him and said, 'Hey, we didn't make that promise. We don't know anything about it.' That immediately caused friction and a problem. They then said, 'Okay, Dennis, if you come in and you once again prove yourself, we'll take care of you.' But here was a guy who was tired of proving himself to the league."

Which was exactly why Rodman had hesitated over joining the team for training camp. "He didn't show up for the first meeting in training camp. Then he came into training camp," Haley said. "We went the first couple of weeks of camp, and he was having negotiations with his attorneys and Popovich, and it almost came to a boiling point. Dennis told them, 'Look, I've already done everything you're asking me to do. I've proven I can play. I've proven I can rebound. What do you care what color my hair is? What do you care if I have tattoos?' I don't think Dennis' appearance really bothered them as much as his offcourt activities and his being late and his rebellion. It became a push-and-shove relationship.

"They took a military stance," Haley said. "Gregg Popovich is a guy who comes from the military and is military-trained. He came in and came with heavy rules and heavy regulations that were gonna confine Dennis from the very beginning."

Rodman's response was to ask repeatedly, "Where's the money you promised me?"

"They said, 'We don't want to deal with that,'" Haley said. "But I think that they took the wrong stance with Dennis in the very first meeting. Dennis is a rebel with a cause, and that cause is to fight authority. So in order to get him to conform to your rules and regulations, you almost have to coddle him like a child and ask him if he'll do something, rather than tell him. If you come to Dennis and say, 'Hey, we need you to be on time, to be part of the team. We need this. Could you do this?' That's great. But if you come to Dennis and you say, 'You be on time or else,' he's gonna test the 'or-else' waters. That was some of the mistakes that they made."

The Spurs' answer to the loggerhead was to suspend Rodman at the start of the season, giving him time away to think over his situation. As a result, he missed the first 17 games of the campaign. As time passed and he lost more and more of his salary, Rodman became resigned to his situation. He felt he had been deceived and lied to, and he hated that. Yet he had no choice but to return. Only there was a complicating factor. Over the summer, he had agreed to pose for nude photographs and to give an interview to *GQ* magazine. In that interview, he had been highly critical of Popovich and new coach Bob Hill (Rodman would later adopt the nickname of "Boner" for Hill). Now, in December, as he was preparing to return, the magazine article was set to be published.

"Dennis came out in the *GQ* article," Haley said. "He knew nothing about Bob Hill. He had never met Bob Hill, and he calls Bob Hill a loser in the GQ article. He said some things about Popovich, and he had never met these people, had never spoken to them. You'll find when dealing with Dennis, his lips move before his mind thinks. He says things, and he feels remorseful for them almost right after he says them. So he went to Bob Hill and apologized for what he said. Before the article actually even hit circulation, Dennis got a copy of it and he read it. He went to Bob Hill and he went to management and he said, 'I'll be honest with you. I didn't know you at the time.'

"It was new management," Haley said. "I think he was a little unhappy with the release of John Lucas, and he was voicing his opinion on something that he hadn't really experienced yet. He let them know it was going to come out, and it's going to be negative press. They told him they didn't have a problem with it."

DEFEAT

Indeed, the Spurs didn't have a problem with Dennis Rodman so long as he buckled down and joined their program, which he sort of did. His return to active status during the holiday rush in December 1994 was wonderfully timed to coincide with a new Nike television spot in which Rodman roughed up and intimidated Santa Claus. The campaign generated an immediate swirl of controversy, which he answered by dying his hair Christmas green with a red symbol for the male sex sketched into his crown.

With radio talk shows still buzzing over Rodman's return, the Spurs embarked on an East Cost road trip after Christmas. He played lethargically against Atlanta in the first game, which infuriated his teammates. They thought he might have been dogging it as a protest over his contract. After the game the Spurs flew to Washington for a game the next night with the Bullets. They awakened the next morning to find the Washington Post offering up a story of league-wide criticism about the Nike ad. "That sends the wrong message to kids," was the gist of the article.

That night, the Spurs met Washington at U.S. Air Arena. For the occasion, Rodman's hair had been redyed a bright orange that had turned the male sex symbol in his crown black. The dye treatments were scalp-searing sessions, but Rodman wanted to take down his Christmas decorations before New Year's.

"I'm the Sunkist man," he told reporters in the locker room before the game.

Actually, his mood was anything but bright. Yet somehow Greg Boeck of *USA Today*, a friendly, familiar face who had first broken the story about Rodman's and Madonna's fling, was able to nudge through his shell to talk.

"Don't call me an athlete," Rodman told Boeck. "Call me an entertainer. I'm a provider of amusement. I'm like a three-ring circus — Barnum & Bailey. Yeah, that's it. Call me Barney."

Certainly, one of Rodman's great assets, outside of his quickness and determination, was his unique sense of humor, something that he shared with Charles Barkley, something that opened both men to being misunderstood. Both had been known for getting into trouble by doing or saying the wrong thing simply because they were trying to get a laugh.

Sensing he had Rodman on a roll, Boeck asked to play a word association game, and Rodman agreed.

Basketball, Boeck said.

"Sex," Rodman answered. "You never forget how to do it."

NBA?

"Lifestyles of the rich and famous."

Rebounding?

"Adversity. I can rebound from any adversity that comes my way."

Commissioner David Stern?

"He's David. I'm Goliath."

John Lucas?

"Motivator."

The Nike/Santa ad?

"Cute. Very cute. I wish people wouldn't take it so seriously."

His current contract, which pays him $2.3 million this season and $2.5 million next?

"Subpar. I paid my dues. I bring lots of excitement, laughter, flash."

Madonna?

"The Mona Lisa. Very beautiful. Very confident. Very unique. There will never be another."

Dennis Rodman?

"The Madonna of the NBA. You'll never see another like me."

Chuck Daly?

"G-O-D."

Discipline?

"Maintain. But there's nothing wrong with throwing some flair as long as you don't hurt anyone."

While Rodman talked with Boeck, the rest of the Spurs sat quietly at their lockers. I asked Terry Cummings, a power forward and a preacher who grew up on the mean streets of Chicago, how it feels to be Rodman's teammate.

"For the most part, Dennis is not an unusual experience to me," Cummings said. "I grew up with Dennises all over Chicago, a lot of people who were different, had their own flair and their own mentality about things. It didn't make it right; it didn't make it wrong. It's just the way they were. The only difference is, is that on a team level, a lot of that stuff just isn't acceptable as when you're out in the streets playing ball."

In some ways, the religious atmosphere of the team has helped the Spurs in dealing with Rodman, and in other ways it has hurt, Cummings said. "It's a good balance. I think the good thing about the people on this team who are Christians is that, you know, we don't waste a whole bunch of time trying to push Jesus on people. You know you live the life and you build relationships with Jesus, and that's how this team is constructed.

"For the most part, I think Dennis has tried really hard," Cummings added. "He really has, you know. You can tell that in the way that it helps the team."

Having finished his interview with Boeck, Rodman sat quietly nearby, his head once again stuffed between headphones that filled his brain with Pearl Jam. I approached him, and he slipped the phones off his ears. I reminded him of my days covering the Pistons, particularly one story I wrote about him in 1989 titled "Air Worm," about his unique basketball skills. (Two years later he will issue his signature basketball shoe and call it Air Worm.)

No problem doing an interview, he said softly. "You want to know when to catch me? I'll just write it down."

He wrote his number on my notepad and told me to make sure to call late. (Several days later, when I phone him at 1 a.m. I will discover that he has not given me his number but Jack Haley's, and that my call awakens Haley's wife, who is in the third trimester of pregnancy. Never much of a Rodman fan anyway, Stacy is furious about his "joke." I am apologetic.)

We chatted for a moment in Washington that night, and I mentioned his struggle with Spurs management.

"Everybody in America knows it's a financial situation," he said.

The conversation ended with security closing the locker room to the media at the allotted 45 minutes before game time. Rodman then headed to the floor, where he stretched a while then turned on his back and pumped bicycles, his legs rotating leisurely in the air. His assistant in all of this was Haley, Rodman's constant companion on the court and off. When they picked up guard Doc Rivers a few weeks ago, the Spurs thought about cutting Haley. But they decided his intangibles were worth keeping, so they chopped Corey Crowder, a free agent.

With Robinson working the post, Chuck Person blasting three pointers, and Rodman executing a rather inspired team defense, the Spurs easily defeated the Bullets that night. The win brought San Antonio's record to

15-10, the first indication that the Spurs were moving past the dysfunction that had possessed them during the first two months of the season. With Rodman back, their defense was especially impressive. Every time the Bullets guards had slipped past Avery Johnson or Vinny Del Negro, Rodman had been there to prevent the easy shot, which had left Bob Hill elated.

"Rodman's help defense is a thing of beauty, isn't it?" I asked the coach afterward. "Dennis knows how to play basketball, believe it or not, at both ends of the floor," Hill replied. "But defensively, if you just take a tape and watch him, his instincts for knowing where the ball is all the time are incredible. He just always knows where the ball is. I think that's one of the reasons he's such a good rebounder.

"He plays great position defense. He's always ready to help. If you get one guy doing that, that's contagious for the team. They start helping one another and trusting one another defensively. That's when you win games."

I asked Hill if Rodman's absence from the team had made coaching him more difficult. "Dennis Rodman and me, we've always gotten along," he said. "I've always had a good relationship with Dennis Rodman. That wasn't between the coach and the players. That was between management and Dennis.

"All the things early in the season that you read and heard were blown out of proportion. We didn't have a special set of rules for Dennis. We never did, and we don't now. All we have are team rules like every other team in the league. Be on time. Come to practice. Lace your shoes up. Put your shirttail in. You know, take your earrings out while you're on the practice floor. Those are just normal rules, and he's done a good job abiding by our rules."

I reminded him of Red Auerbach, the great Boston coach, who had a special treatment for his great center Bill Russell. Essentially, Russell didn't have to practice if he didn't want to, and that must not have hurt because the Celtics won 11 championships in 13 years. Would a special set of rules work for Rodman? I asked.

"No," Hill said quickly. "That would be a dangerous thing. That's what happened last year, and that's why the team disintegrated, and that's why they got beat in the playoffs. You know as we move along here in professional basketball, it's my opinion that these franchises have become multimillion dollar corporations, and with the investments that we're making in the players, and with the money that the league is making, I think it behooves all of us to try and run these teams more like a corporation. The 12 players are the most important people in the corporation. When you're making that kind of money, and you're being commercialized as they are, I think they have a responsibility to give something back to the organizations that made them what they are. That's my philosophy."

Inside the locker room, Dennis sat icing his knees down, his head phones on, waving off anyone who approached for an interview. A small boy stepped up cautiously and presented a copy of the book *Rebound* for an autograph. Rodman silently took the book, looked away and signed his name in broad strokes.

Nearby, guard Avery Johnson answered a question about the Spurs' growing confidence.

"This is the best talent on the team that we've ever assembled," Johnson said. "I'm more mature. Dave's more mature. Sean Elliot (who has been traded back to the Spurs from the Pistons) is, too. We got a veteran ball club, so we have to win a championship in the next two or three years."

What do you think of Dennis' help defense? I asked him.

"I think it's great," he said. "Sometimes guys relax a little too much when he gets in the game with the rebounding. We just tend to fall asleep because he's so good on defense."

David Robinson, who had been struggling with a sprained ankle, stood nearby chatting with a group of local reporters. Washington was his hometown. He had gone to high school in the Virginia suburbs and attended college at nearby Annapolis. After two months of vexation, he was starting to see that the Spurs could be pretty good. "We have a strong group," he said.

Is this team having fun yet? I asked him, pointing out that Dennis was back, but there seemed to be an air of uneasiness about the Spurs.

"I don't think we're having fun," he admitted. "As much as we want to just yet. At the beginning of the season it was tough. We weren't really enjoying things at all. We were struggling. Now it's coming a little bit better. I think we have a better understanding of what we want to accomplish, especially defensively. Now, obviously we're putting points on the board, but we have to get better offensively."

Is it necessary to have fun? I asked.

"No question," he replied with a slight smile. "If you're not having fun, you're doing something wrong. Especially winning. When you win, it's fun. You win three out of four games in this league, you're gonna be having a lot of fun. We're trying to get to that point."

One of the big keys to getting there is Rodman, he said. "It's tough for him, but he's gonna get there, obviously, and when he does, we're gonna be all right. He's a guy you can have at the end of the game. He's gonna get boards for you. He's gonna make smart plays. Offensively, he passes real well. He's gonna be good."

With Rodman out, the Spurs had struggled to prove they could win big without him. "Especially early in the season," Robinson said. "When we went through some of those losses, it was tough. But guys didn't complain, didn't get on each other. They showed a lot of character when we were down, and now that we're starting to win some, guys at least have an established relationship and can trust each other now. I think we're starting to build something good. We got a new coach, a new system, some new players. It's not easy to jump right in, but we like what we see here in this locker room. We got some good veteran players. We're going in the right direction."

Outside the locker room, I encountered Jack Haley. How's Dennis doing? I asked. "Some nights he's in a really good mood and ready to go," he said. "Tonight he was really tired. We had a back-to-back games, and today we had a lot of things we had to take care of. But when he's on the floor and having a good time, things go well. In San Antonio the other night, he had 20 rebounds and was hyping the crowd. He was his old self. He's just gotta have a lot of fun. When he has fun, he's one of the best players in the league.

"Bob Hill and Dennis are establishing a good relationship," he added. "They're starting to grow and become better friends as well as coach and player. His relationship with management is good now. It's more distant and also hands-off. If they give Dennis more space, then everything will work out. He loves the city of San Antonio. He loves it there, and they love him. He's a god in San Antonio. Anywhere he goes, the fans worship him. He loves it there. He doesn't want to go anywhere."

What about the emphasis on a corporate atmosphere? Will Dennis be able to handle that? I asked.

"The Spurs are really moving toward making it a family-oriented game," Haley said. "If you look at the attendance, it's a lot of families. What Dennis brings to the floor, if done properly, is great for families. They don't mind the earrings. They don't mind the orange hair, the colorful hair. It's the little things that he does sometimes that are negative to the game that they're worried about. But he's really changed that; he's cleaned it up. They haven't had those incidents this year."

I looked at Haley's face to see if he really believed what he was saying, but I couldn't tell. Moments later, Haley and Rodman posed for photos outside the locker room with David Robinson's brother. For the moment at least, everything seemed a picture of peace with this team. In fact, time would reveal that the Spurs had just embarked on a series of win streaks that would lift them to a league-best 62-win finish for the regular season. They would be able to do this despite losing Rodman again in March, this time to a separated shoulder from a motorcycle wreck (it would prove a mere speed bump on his highway to hell). When he returned from injury they resumed their winning ways, with their armada of three-point shooters keeping the floor spread so that Robinson could work in the post and with Rodman giving them a toughness defensively and on the boards.

Ultimately, though, even the winning couldn't mask the fundamental problems with the San Antonio Spurs.

First, Rodman's differences with management dogged the team like a running skirmish over the winter and spring of 1995. The Spurs had their rules, and Rodman answered with an insurrection that cost him tens of thousands of dollars in fines.

"They were fining him $500 and they were fining him every single game," Haley would later confide. "I'm talking about every single day, $500 a day. Because Dennis made a concentrated effort to be late. It was his way of sticking it in their side.

"I pulled up one day to practice. He's sitting there 15 minutes early for practice. I said, 'C'mon, let's go.' He said, 'I'm listening to some Pearl Jam.' He walks into practice 25 minutes late. It was almost his way of saying, 'You're not going to control me. I'm gonna be one minute, two minutes late, every single day.'"

Rodman's other great conflict was with his teammates. At times, with the religious fervor of several key figures, the Spurs' team meetings would seem to be almost prayer meetings. Rodman, though, was as freewheeling about his spiritual life as he was his social calendar. To say the least, it was an odd fit of personalities.

"The religious aspect was not so much a problem for Dennis as it was for the guys on the team who were very religious," Haley said. "David Robinson, Terry Cummings, Avery Johnson, I mean these guys are very, very, very religious, and the things Dennis did bothered them. The little things Dennis did got under their skin and caused a lot of internal problems."

Yet perhaps the primary problem for the San Antonio Spurs was Rodman's belief that David Robinson lacked commitment as an athlete. "Dennis had a real problem in his respect for David Robinson as a player,"

Haley later explained. "He had problems with David's intensity and work ethic in practice. One thing about Dave. Dave could be the most talented player and athlete in the NBA. Dave is probably the greatest athlete in the game. Dave can go out and get 30 points and 12 rebounds without putting forth a real effort. He's that good. Therefore, he's not a big practice guy. Not a big work ethic guy. By (January), Dave would have sat out 30 practices. It's tendinitis. It's, 'I'm sore today.' Whatever it was, Dennis is a practice guy, and it didn't sit well with Dennis. That caused a lot of their problems, just work ethic.

"Dave and I are very good friends," Haley added. "I'm not knocking him in any way. I admire him. He was the MVP in 1995. I still would vote for him for the MVP. He deserved it."

Yet Rodman wasn't the only Spur who had had problems with Robinson's work ethic. Ironically, though, veteran forward Terry Cummings had been bothered by Robinson's approach in previous seasons. Cummings said that in 1994-95, Robinson was finally showing real signs of maturing.

"He just wasn't focused, wasn't committed, when he first got here," Cummings said. "He didn't have to be. He had a whole lot of money, and his mind was on other things. But he's gotten more focused. He got married, and then he became more focused. Even before he got married, actually the year before he was starting to really focus on basketball, when he played the game. But this is the most focused he's been the last couple of years."

Rodman, however, was not impressed with Robinson's cavalier attitude about practice, so he withheld conversation from the center and team captain like a parent withholds approval from a child. He went to extreme efforts to make it clear that he had nothing to say to Robinson. The more effort Rodman made not to speak, the more determined Robinson became to establish communication.

"Dave tried everything," Haley said. "He tried everything imaginable to bond with Dennis Rodman, to get through with Dennis Rodman to form a friendship. I'm good friends with Dennis and I'm good friends with Dave. Dave would ask me, 'Why don't the three of us go to lunch? Why don't we sit down and try to talk?' He would try to talk to Dennis about basketball to form a bond. Dennis wouldn't respond. Dave is very religious. He felt that part of his quest was to get through to Dennis Rodman on a religious level, to try to turn his life around. That didn't work out at all. That caused some conflict. I admire Dave. Again, you're a grown man; you're one of the richest guys in the NBA; you keep going to someone and try to get through to them, and the person continues to snub you. . . I admire the guy for continuing to try. I would have thrown in the towel and said, 'Hey, F.U.'

"But he continued to try to be a man and a leader," Haley said, "so for that I admire Dave."

Even their opportunity to make money together — which Rodman badly needed — wasn't enough to break his will. When the two made a commercial for Pizza Hut that emphasized their basic personality differences, Rodman was amazingly cordial before the camera and just as amazingly chilly off the set. "They flew on their pizza commercial on a three or four hour flight on a private plane," Haley said. "They never spoke. Dennis would put his head phones on and never speak to or from.

"The only time that Dave and Dennis would have any conversation would be in a game on the floor, or in practice regarding a direct basketball play. As far as socially, or off the floor, or anything of that nature, there was no social interaction whatsoever."

Robinson's every attempt at social intercourse was met with one unbearably awkward response after another, even so despite Haley's best efforts to bring the two closer. "We were trying to build a bond with Dave and Dennis, and I was trying to help," Haley said. "We went to my restaurant in Southern California, Captain Jack's. We had gone to L.A. for a game. Dave and Vinny Del Negro hop in one limousine and drive down to the restaurant. Dennis and I are in another limousine. We follow them down to my father's restaurant. We get to Captain Jack's. Dennis and I are laughing and talking the whole way, bubbly in the limousine. We walk into the restaurant. The second we walk in, Dennis goes into his clamshell. The four of us — four teammates — sit there and have a two and a half hour dinner, and in two and a half hours the only words muttered by Dennis Rodman were nods and single-word answers. 'Dennis, how was your food tonight?' 'Great.' Guys would ask him a question, he would just nod or he would give one-syllable answers. Vinny and Dave went out of their way to get him involved in the conversation. I tried. He sat there and stared off in space or watched TV. He facilitates 90 percent of the problems that come his way."

Because the Spurs kept winning, it was easy enough for Robinson to be philosophical about his difficulties. He badly wanted to win a championship and hoped that maybe the Spurs could pull it off despite their lack of chemistry.

Yet other people close to the situation could only wonder. What would happen when the playoffs arrived, when the pressure got turned up to unbearable levels? Who would bear up under it? Who would break? More important, what would Dennis Rodman and David Robinson have to say to each other then?

QUICK NICK TO THE RESCUE

January 11, 1995 — Charlotte Coliseum

The fan in the front row at the Charlotte Coliseum doesn't know it yet, but he's about to make Nick Van Exel's night. It's another tough road game, and Van Exel, the Lakers' precocious second-year point guard, has started slowly. Early in the first quarter, with his energy level seemingly stuck in low gear, he begins searching the sidelines for a lift.

And there, on the front row, he finds just the guy to do the trick. Best of all, the fan is a brother, one who knows how to talk a little trash. "You're selling out, Nick!" the brother yells. "It's gonna be a long ride home, baby!"

That's my man, Van Exel thinks.

And with that, the plucky young guard begins a "conversation," a verbal battle with his heckler. To counter the fan's barrage of insults, Van Exel uses chest-thumping, self-congratulatory displays and a full array of grins, quick comments, and sideways looks.

All of which are met by the brother's relentless reminder: "You're selling out, Nick."

Finally, just before he's about to shoot a free throw, Van Exel turns, grabs his crotch, tugs at it and nods defiantly at the heckler. The message is clear: "Bite me."

It sends a ripple of laughter through the courtside seats. Even the brother can't suppress a grin. "You're selling out, Nick," he answers lamely.

To the contrary, Van Exel seems to have shaken off his road weariness and is now fully energized. The mind game firmly in control, the young guard drives the Lakers to a steady comeback. In the fourth quarter with Charlotte holding a narrow lead, he faces full-court pressure from Muggsy Bogues, the Hornets' muscular little point guard whose quickness is a nightmare for most guards in the league. But not for Van Exel. Left to bring the ball up alone against Bogues' pressure, Van Exel looks smugly at his defender, does two quick jab steps, then pirouettes and zips away, leaving the NBA's supposedly quickest man sitting dumfounded.

At midcourt, Charlotte's Dell Curry attempts to step in and pick Van Exel up, but the Laker guard merely does a spin dribble — a majestically graceful 360-degree move — right around him and keeps motoring straight to the basket, where Hornets center Alonzo Mourning awaits. Mourning seems surprised that the 6-1, 170-pound Van Exel keeps coming. The surprise then spills into full disbelief when the guard rises up right in the center's face and flips in a layup. Van Exel has gone end to end, first blowing off the quickest, then challenging the most ferocious. The result, as you might expect, is devastating for the Hornets. Once seemingly in control of the game, they stumble.

With 20 seconds to go, Bogues fouls Van Exel, who makes a free throw to push the Laker lead to 106-102.

"Damn you, Nick," the brother in the front row yells hoarsely.

Moments later, the game ends, and, as Van Exel heads off, the fan yells, "Nick." Van Exel turns around, and the brother points at him and smiles. Van Exel points back and grins.

"On the court, when he gets into a conversation with the fans, that motivates him," Lakers rookie guard Eddie Jones says of Van Exel. "That motivates him every night. I'm like, 'Nick, shut up!' Off the court, he's calm and quiet, but on the court he's like a different person."

"On the road, it seems I play a lot better when I have somebody harassing me," Van Exel says, smiling. "I like that. It gets me fired up. It's fun. We were getting on each other during the game. He was saying things. I was saying things. But when it was all said and done, we pointed at each other and said goodbye. It's all in fun."

Tremendous fun, unless you happen to be the home team faced with the challenge of the Lakers' brilliant young guards. Van Exel possesses a nearly indefensible quickness, and Jones has the long arms to snatch the ball right out the passing lanes, which gives opponents stress attacks as they try to work their offenses against the Lakers' pressure.

"These guys are truly amazing," says Laker assistant Larry Drew.

Perhaps the most amazing thing about this new edition of the Lakers is how quickly and brilliantly Laker executive Jerry West has rebuilt them from the ashes of the great Laker Showtime teams featuring coach Pat Riley, Magic Johnson, Kareem Abdul-Jabbar, James Worthy and Byron Scott (teams that won five NBA championships). West had been displeased with how unorganized the team seemed to be under coach Randy Pfund in 1993-94. Pfund had, of course, countered that the club was clearly one in transition, that it was impossible to get much more out of the roster than he did. James Worthy, in particular, struggled with his declining skills and with his waning passion for the game. Trading him, however, had become an impossibility because of the balloon contract with which team owner Jerry Buss had rewarded him, a deal that paid him a reported $7 million per season over the final two years of the agreement.

The Lakers had somehow managed to make the '93 playoffs and give the Phoenix Suns fits before losing in the first round, which was just enough to save Pfund's job. But the 1993-94 season was doomed to be yet another phase of transition. In the '93 draft, West went for North Carolina forward George Lynch with the 12th pick of the first round, but the real prize proved to be Van Exel out of the University of Cincinnati with the 37th selection in the second round.

Most pro scouts had seen talent in Van Exel but worried about his shot selection and questioned his attitude and character. Part of the problem stemmed from Van Exel's seeming reluctance to visit certain teams that were interested in him, including Charlotte.

West has often said that if you don't have a top pick you have to wait around and hope that other people make mistakes. With Van Exel, the entire NBA made a mistake in 1993. It could be argued that even West wasn't aware that he had gotten a star. But soon after Van Exel came to work, the Lakers realized they had a rare, rare find, a rookie who could start and excel at point guard.

He was, however, just that — a rookie — and that had contributed to an immense problem for Pfund. The Lakers began the season with a starting lineup that averaged just 23.4 years in age, the youngest in the league. Plus, the team still lacked strong rebounding and a leader. West had hoped that Lynch, whose defense and rebounding had helped Carolina to the '93 NCAA title, would contribute in those areas. But Pfund seemed unimpressed with the rookie, who had a power forward's game in a small forward's body. The Lakers needed scoring and rebounding from the small forward slot, and Lynch's jump shot was suspect. But where Lynch struggled, Van Exel immediately found a comfort zone and a job as the team's starting point guard.

Unfortunately, the roster was strangely unmotivated, which frustrated both rookies, not to mention Pfund. The Lakers opened the season with a losing month, then proceeded to stack up the kind of forlorn defeats not seen since their dark days in Minneapolis. "It's tough," Van Exel had confided during his first season. "There are a lot of games where we go out and see guys who really don't want to play and are not giving their all. That really hurts the most because we know they can do better."

Sitting and watching this lack of effort was particularly tough on the immensely proud and workmanlike Lynch. "George didn't lose many games in his college career, and he's won a national championship," Van Exel said. "It was hard for him losing so many games. He felt there were a lot of games where we should have won, where people should have tried harder."

Ultimately, the thing that worked in Lynch's favor was a run of injuries that forced Pfund to play him. Given time, he showed a knack for offensive rebounds and putbacks and defensive energy. Some still doubted that he would ever possess the skills of an NBA starter, but it became clear that he was a strong bench player, the kind of frontcourt depth the laconic Lakers badly needed. Most important, he had intensity.

Yet when a team has to draw on rookies for its strength, there's trouble. And there was plenty of that for Pfund. Strangely, the Lakers picked March, the team's only month with a winning record, to release the second-year coach. In a move typically classy of Buss and West, they first extended his contract an additional year in early March, although their decision was already made. From there, the Lakers went on a rare winning streak, claiming a 6-1 record from March 7 up to their March 23 game against the Mavericks, before which management relieved Pfund and assistant Chet Kammerer of their duties.

For two games, longtime Laker assistant Bill Bertka ran the team until new coach Magic Johnson and assistant Michael Cooper could get situated. The emotion and excitement of Johnson's return generated renewed interest in the Great Western Forum, where ticket sales had sagged through the miserable season. Those feelings grew when Magic won five of his first six games. Yet it soon became clear that his presence on the bench was a halfhearted experiment, and the problems that had plagued the Lakers remained very malignant.

The end of the season was quite ugly, a 10-game losing streak, the longest in franchise history. The losing gained momentum after Johnson announced that he wouldn't take the job on a long-term basis. Frustrated by the lack of concern among key players, Johnson reportedly smashed a player's beeper against a wall when it went off during practice. He wanted full commitment to winning, and they weren't willing to make it. Johnson himself wasn't ready to take on the challenge and stress of coaching. Instead, he acquired a minority ownership of the team and settled in as a vice president not long after the Lakers finished 33-49 and out of the playoffs for the first time in almost two decades.

Someone else, it seems, would have to do the coaching.

For that, West turned to Del Harris, a well-traveled veteran known for his slowdown offenses. Actually Harris had been a proponent of the push game during his days in Houston. But he slowed down the Rockets' offense to match the skills of then-center Moses Malone, and that resulted in a trip to the 1981 NBA Finals against the Boston Celtics. The Rockets lost, but Harris' record for flexibility was established among keen observers. Which is why West could hire him with a clear conscience before the 1994-95 season. West knew that Harris wasn't wed to any one system and would find the style of play suited to the young roster.

The other big holes for the Lakers were a small forward who could score and rebound consistently and a superstar. West found both in a deal with Phoenix that brought in Cedric Ceballos, a fifth-year forward with a rapidly developing game.

Added to that was the selection of Eddie Jones out of Temple with the tenth overall pick in the '94 draft. Chicago Bulls general manager Jerry Krause had badly wanted Jones. In fact, Krause's real effort in attempting to trade forward Scottie Pippen for Seattle power forward Shawn Kemp in 1994 was to get into position to draft Eddie Jones. The Pippen/Kemp deal fell through, however, and Jones fell to the Lakers. Teamed with Van Exel at the point, Ceballos at small forward, Elden Campbell at power forward and Vlade Divac at center, Jones proved he could contribute immediately as the Lakers' off guard. As a result, they were one of the NBA's big surprises in 1994-95.

That was especially true of the development of the young guard tandem. "We're one of the best teams in the league," the 57-year-old Harris said unabashedly eight weeks into the season. "I think Nick and Eddie Jones have got to be the most exciting backcourt in the league," he added. "I mean these kids are 23 years old and they play like salty veterans. We are really blessed."

Jones says that away from the game Van Exel is a quiet sort who likes listening to music, playing video games and going to movies. Off the court, about the only time Van Exel gets riled is if he sees a teammate staying out too late or engaging in behavior detrimental to the team.

Then Van Exel doesn't hesitate to confront that player, even if it involves an older veteran. This policing is an extension of Van Exel's natural leadership abilities. But it also comes at the urging Johnson, who used to run the team with the same intensity.

Since Johnson's abrupt retirement in 1991, the Lakers had drifted along without a leader. That helps explain why Van Exel's intense competitiveness and leadership abilities were so welcomed in Los Angeles. "He's very competitive," said assistant coach Larry Drew. "If you find a guy with a passion to win, you got yourself something special. Hopefully he can pass that will to win on to some of these other guys. Nick's very passionate. He wants to win badly and gets frustrated when he doesn't."

"I got a lot of competitive relatives," Van Exel said of his hunger. "All of my aunts, when they were growing up, played softball and were great competitors. My Dad, my uncles, everybody in my family always wanted to win."

The leadership abilities weren't exactly an acquired facet of his personality but something Van Exel wanted to develop. "He came in this season really focused on trying to lead," Drew said. "And he did a good job. Our players look at him as a leader. He has commanded that kind of respect. He's demanded it, too."

"I think he's a great floor leader," said teammate Anthony Peeler. "The Lakers gave him the ball as a rookie and told him to run the team. This year he's had a lot of things on his shoulders, a lot of pressure from everybody, to see if he can do well. He's proven that he can. He's focused as a leader. In the hotel on the road, if you're hanging out too late, he'll go to the player and pinpoint 'em. That's what we need in a captain. He's letting everybody know he's a leader.

"Last year as a rookie, Nick was just witnessing a lot of stuff that he couldn't really do anything about. This year he's taken it upon himself to really get eye contact and really get inside each player on the team."

At least part of the motivation for this leadership effort stemmed from Van Exel's frequent talks with Johnson. "Magic's very inspirational," Van Exel said. "The rule we have about night life is that you can go out as long as you're ready on the court to handle your business and be professional. The Lakers gave me a lot of confidence last year to be the leader, and it's a role I want."

As Drew pointed out when other players struggled with the leadership mantle following Johnson's retirement, the efforts to lead the team only work if you have the talent and competitiveness to make it stick. In that regard, Van Exel's quickness is a key factor because it makes him a unique player. "I call him 'Quick.' That's his nickname," Peeler said, "because nobody in the NBA can keep up with him right now. They had a year during his rookie season to see him. But now they're trying to use the excuse that they didn't know he had all of these moves. But this year they know. They've scouted him, and they still can't stop him. I'm waiting to see if there is somebody in the league who can keep up with him. Nick's been going up against the best guards in the league all season, and I haven't seen one of them take the ball away from him yet, or stop him. He's just doing what he wants to right now. He knows he's good."

"The thing that first opened my eyes about Nick Van Exel," Larry Drew said, "is how easily he broke the defender down. That's something that few point guards can do. You find a lot who have the speed to blow by defenders. But actually breaking them down off the dribble with your moves is another matter. Nick's doing it time and time again. And once he breaks them down, he knows what to do once he gets around them. He came to me at the start of this season and said, 'Did I shoot the ball too much last year?' (Van Exel led the team in field goal attempts but only shot 39 percent from the floor as a rookie.) Personally, I didn't think he did, because it's so easy for him to get around a defender and make things happen in a transition game. He finds himself open for a lot of shots. You gotta take those shots.

"You look at the point guards today, most are scoring guards. If you find one who can score and distribute the ball, you got yourself something special. In Nick, we have something special."

Sometimes, Van Exel admitted, he surprises even himself with his moves and quickness. "I play a lot on instinct," he said. "Sometimes when I do a move, I think, 'I never did that before.'"

The summer after his rookie season, Van Exel spent his time in the LA summer leagues focusing on becoming a better distributor. "I wanted to get the ball to guys in scoring position," he explained. "I wanted to learn to set guys up and work on staying focused and running a team, being in control of a game."

Peeler swears that Van Exel, who has been rewarded with a handsome contract, is using his draft-day slight as motivation to drive the Lakers to road win after road win, and the other teams around the league are discovering paybacks are hell. "He's coming out wanting to destroy every team that overlooked him," Peeler said. "He doesn't talk about it. He just goes out there and does it."

"I guess they'll hold it against me forever," Van Exel says, implying that other teams harbor a grudge against him because of the draft. This, of course, is obviously disingenuous. It is Van Exel himself who seems intent on showing the rest of the league that he has a long, long memory.

Regardless of its origin, Van Exel's motivation keeps Del Harris immensely pleased, although player and coach had to overcome an early season misunderstanding. Harris quickly downplayed a playing time disagreement they had during a game in Portland. The incident, Harris said, "was a nothing kind of situation. I love working with him. He's a special player. It's amazing to watch him get better all the time. Tougher. More heads up. The guy can beat you every way. He can score outside, inside, make the play off the dribble. He works on the defender and is good off the ball, too. He's terrific."

Both Harris and West offered similar endorsement of Jones, who at 6-6, 190, has the body and temperament to play both big guard and small forward. Guard, however, is his first position, because he has the size to post up opponents. The Lakers spent much of his rookie season building his confidence and skills, with Drew schooling him on his mid range jumper and Cooper teaching the nuances of tough defense and stopping the pick and roll.

The confidence building began the moment Jones was drafted. "Jerry West came to me several times and said, 'Man, you can be great,'" Jones recalled. "He's like THE basketball guru, the best of scouts. So that just made me want to work harder over the summer so I could come here and perform to his level of expectation. I just tried to do my best to play my heart out."

There was little question that Jones did that, although his coaches thought he was too reckless in taking the ball to the basket and challenging the league's bigger, stronger inside players. Sure enough, Jones' fine rookie season was interrupted when he injured a shoulder dunking. Losing his scoring and defense could have been disastrous, except that Peeler, long in management's doghouse and slowed by a series of injuries, came through with a tremendous spring.

After leaving Charlotte, the young Lakers closed out the schedule with a show of strength, winning 48 games and finishing in fifth place in their conference.

At the height of the excitement, Van Exel was asked if it was the most fun he'd ever had in basketball. "It's not the most fun in my life," he said. "Not yet. I think that's still to come."

That seemed a promising enough forecast for the Lakers. More good times ahead. Brought on by a tough little guy who likes to search the sidelines for a motivational ploy. Will it be enough to bring more championships? If Van Exel's heart has anything to do with, the answer will be affirmative.

"He's got that burning desire to win," Drew said of Van Exel. "You just don't teach that. It has to come from within."

HOOPS BY THE NUMBERS

FEBRUARY 1995

If only the National Basketball Association could suspend its rules for a season and adopt some fantasy league guidelines. You know, the kind of deal where players can score points for all of their assists, steals and rebounds. Maybe that would work for the Utah Jazz. Maybe then they could win the championship that John Stockton and Karl Malone and coach Jerry Sloan so badly crave.

There's no telling how many fantasy titles Stockton and Malone, the game's premiere point guard and power forward, have delivered over the years for the stat freaks in the fantasy leagues. Probably a thousand.

Imagine that, a thousand championships.

And the Utah Jazz only want one.

It seems a shame that a team so rich in numbers hasn't been able to add them all up to that one title. After all, Stockton and Malone are well into their tenth season playing together. And by all accounts, they've acquitted themselves remarkably well.

For example, coach Jerry Sloan says that each and every of those 10 seasons Stockton and Malone have come into camp in impeccable shape. Which helps explain why they each have missed a total of only four games over that 10 seasons.

Four games each. Think about it. Maybe the NBA should declare a special exception and award the 1995 trophy based solely on things like consistency, dedication and work ethic. Then Stockton and Malone would be primo contenders, because nobody in pro basketball goes harder than those two.

"I've been very lucky," Sloan says. "I don't think anybody in the coaching business could be more fortunate than I am, to have two guys like that."

For that reason, Sloan says he wants to take care not to push Stockton, who is 33, and Malone, 32, too hard. "We'd like to preserve these guys for as long as we can," the coach says, "for what they've given us."

Needless to say, Stockton and Malone don't exactly share that concern for the future. They want the world championship, and they want it now.

NIGHT IN, NIGHT OUT

The scenes repeat themselves almost every night.

An opponent takes a bad shot, and instantly Malone releases upcourt. Underneath, Jazz forward David Benoit grabs the defensive rebound and contemplates for a fraction of a second what to do with it. Stockton rushes up to demand the ball. Benoit gives it up, and Stockton immediately hurls it the length of the floor, where it falls into Malone's waiting hands just two steps from the hoop for the easy layup.

Ker-ching. Stockton and Malone ring up another two points, another assist. How perfectly numerical that in the season that Stockton closes in on 10,000 assists and the league's all-time assist record, Malone is busy logging his 20,000th point.

Moments later, the Jazz are running their halfcourt offense. Malone is posted on the left side of the lane. The slightest crease of a passing lane opens, and Malone turns his massive 6-9, 256-pound body just enough to pin the defender on his hip. Stockton threads the bounce pass low and away, so that only Malone can reach it. He scoops it up like gravy and pivots. Ker-ching. Another easy layup. Another assist.

Then there's Stockton on the break, moving full speed, with his head turning like a swivel, surveying the options, seeing who's with him on the wings. Stockton keeps pushing and penetrates and then does what every coach tells a point guard not to do: He leaves his feet. In mid air, he looks hard right to the deep corner where Benoit awaits the pass. But at the last instant, Stockton flips the ball back over his left shoulder, across the key to where Malone is posted up for an open jumper. Ker-ching.

"There's a comfort level with Karl," Stockton says later. "He's got great hands. There doesn't have to be that big of a gap to get him the ball. He can catch it. He can get himself in position. With that, there's a lot of confidence in the passes you throw him."

Confidence, indeed. Stockton is in the process of leading the NBA in assists for an unprecedented eighth straight season. Oscar Robertson led the league six times but never more than three seasons in a row.

Stockton also holds the record for assists in a season (1,164 in 1990-91). Only nine times in league history has a player totalled more than

1,000 assists. Seven of those seasons belong to Stockton and he is in the process of stacking up his eighth.

Conversely, Malone is well on his way to racking up his eighth consecutive season of 2,000 points scored, which leads to the inevitable questions about who is more responsible for this success, Stockton or Malone?

The answer, of course, is that they both are.

Their accomplishments are truly impressive for two players who didn't earn scholarships to big-time colleges and weren't selected as lottery picks in the NBA draft. Malone, who went to Louisiana Tech, was taken by the Jazz with the 13th pick of the first round of the 1986 draft.

Stockton, who played college ball at Gonzaga in Spokane, Washington, near the neighborhood bar that his parents run, was taken with the 16th pick in 1984. "John never started out as the best player in his age group," his father Jack recalled last year. "But he was always gaining on everybody. And there were some tremendous matches with the older boys. That's when I started seeing it coming. John never got beat the same way twice. They'd pop around him pretty good. But the next day they'd have to find another way to beat him."

Despite the fact that they keep relentlessly stacking up their superior numbers, both Stockton and Malone hate talking about them.

You can hear the disdain in Stockton's voice at their mere mention. You talk numbers, he sneers. Throughout January and February, as he closed in on the NBA's all-time assist mark held by Magic Johnson, he gave his media questioners the same blank look and the same pat response when they asked about his milestone.

"It's just a stat," he said. "It's not winning and it's not losing."

He paused to inhale a bit to help hold back whatever urge he had to say something else. Stockton is good at holding his tongue. His replies to interviews are as spare and to-the-point as his floor game.

Although not as terse, Malone holds a similar view of his individual achievements. "I'm in this thing for one reason," he says, "and that's to win it."

They're right, of course. Numbers are for losers and also-rans. Numbers are a salve for people who don't win championships. Stockton and Malone don't want a salve.

Over the past months, as Stockton steadily moved up the all-time assist standings, passing Bob Cousy, Isiah Thomas, Oscar Robertson and finally Magic, reporters would ask him what it was like to join their special company. "I don't know if it puts me in their company or not," he would reply. "Those guys are all something special."

What he meant, of course, is that Cousy, Robertson, Thomas and Johnson all played on at least one championship team. For all of their numbers, Stockton and Malone don't have the only validation that truly matters.

In the 1992 Olympics, when Stockton played with Johnson on Dream Team I, the Utah playmaker had only one question for the great Laker floor leader: "How did you win all those championships?"

THE BIG RIDDLE

Indeed, solving that riddle has driven this pair to near distraction. The situation boiled over just before the 1994 All Star game in Minneapolis Malone angrily questioned management's commitment in a meeting with Jazz owner Larry Miller. "I don't have 10 years left in this league and I don't want 10 years," Malone later said. "I want to win it in Utah. But if you don't show me as management that you do, I know some teams that I want to play for.

"They gotta prove to me by attempting to sign players or something to win, and not just players out of the CBA and stuff like that. My whole thing is, I hate to hear, 'I'm trying. We're trying.' Why is it that we're trying and everybody else is doing?"

Management quietly gritted their teeth through Malone's barrage, but within weeks they made a deal to acquire shooting guard Jeff Hornacek. Although he came late, Hornacek and the rapid improvement of center Felton Spencer made the Jazz a force by the 1994 playoffs. They battled their way to the Western Conference Finals against the Houston Rockets, only to find Malone greatly weakened by a vicious flu bug.

Strangely, Jazz owner Larry Miller stormed around complaining that Malone wasn't giving a full effort, leading to a riotous blowup within the organization in the wake of their 4-1 loss to the Rockets. Again talk of a Malone trade surfaced and stayed around through much of the summer.

Amazingly, the team was able to mend by the start of the '94-95 schedule, and the first full season with Hornacek plus the addition of backup forwards Antoine Carr and Adam Keefe has meant that the Jazz are more competitive than ever, going so far as to stack up a 15-game road winning streak in January and February that came just one shy of breaking the all-time record set by the 1972 Lakers.

Always good at executing offensively, Stockton and Malone became even better with Hornacek's outside shooting serving to spread out the defense.

Sadly, just as the Jazz were hitting their stride, misfortune again struck. Felton Spencer, whose defense and rebounding were critical to their success, went down with a season-ending achilles tendon injury, leaving Utah without a true center.

Regardless, the Jazz have kept up their winning ways and stayed in the thick of the heated Western Conference wars, where Houston, San Antonio, Phoenix, Utah and Seattle all have their hearts set on a title.

"Guys have to keep playing hard," Malone says. "That's the important thing. If we do that, we should be fine."

INTANGIBLES PLUS

Playing hard doesn't seem to be a question for Utah, with Stockton and Malone providing the lead.

"They're superstars who are down home," says 11-year veteran Antoine Carr, who came to Utah just before the season opened. "I mean I've run across a lot of guys in this league who thought they were better than everybody else and kind of carried themselves that way. But these guys are normal guys. They like to go fishing, hunting. They hang out together, do those things together. I've never really seen superstars like that."

Adam Keefe, who came to Utah in a September trade from Atlanta, said he was surprised when his new superstar teammates phoned to see if he needed help moving in. "The first thing that struck me," Keefe says, "is the type of people they are. They're completely unpretentious. They both do such a great job of keeping their lives in perspective."

The atmosphere that Stockton and Malone set around the Jazz makes it easier for the lesser players to find their confidence, Keefe says. "The important thing about their leadership is that they're not spokesmen; they're not flamboyant characters. They lead by their actions on the court, by demonstrating through their intensity and work ethic.

"Neither one of them will ever be late for a bus, a practice or a game. Neither one of them will ever cut corners in practice. In that sense they never take advantage of the special position they're in, and that's what makes them so tremendous."

This stands in stark contrast to Keefe's experience in Atlanta, playing alongside Dominique Wilkins. "For me, especially, what a difference, coming from where I came from," he says. "Here, they appreciate and understand the small things that get done. Karl's great. If you set a pick for him to get him open, he'll say, 'Thanks.'

"They understand what it takes, that it's not the world revolving around them on the basketball court, that they need other components out there. They're both phenomenal in that sense. They're not concerned with how they're seen in the big picture, if they drive the nicest cars or have the most flamboyant clothing. That doesn't appeal to them. What appeals to them are the basics of life — and winning."

Malone, who owns a tractor-trailer which he drives in the offseason, says he likes to think of a quote he read by Dallas Cowboys quarterback Troy Aikman about how it's important to walk with your teammates, not out in front of them. "Everybody talks about the superstar status," Malone says. "I don't know how they're supposed to act. That's not how I was brought up. If we were horses behinds, there'd be total chaos in this locker room.

"It's great when the coach calls your play, and you make a pass to your teammate. That's your play, and you can do anything you want with it. All of a sudden, your teammates say, 'I feel a part of this.' And that's what it's all about. It's not about me, me, me. It's about us, and that's the only way I know how to be."

And that is why, to a man, the Jazz are focused on a single goal. "If you watch the way we play," Antoine Carr says, "the guys are all high-fiving from one to 12. That's something special. You don't get that very often.

"We're gonna try as hard as we can to do what Karl wants to do and what John wants to do, which is win the championship."

That, of course, would be just perfect, because when everything is said and done, Stockton and Malone will be able to sit by a fishing hole someplace and have a little fun making sense of all those grand, glorious numbers.

AIRBALLS IN THE DESERT

PHOENIX, ARIZONA, FEBRUARY 8-11, 1995

In the old days, it was a drab little event, mostly ignored by the fans and the media, but the NBA All Star Weekend has grown into a wonderfully overstuffed affair in recent seasons. Now, it's a vapid, superhyped array of nothingness, a weekend of parties and open bars and behind-the-scenes wheeling and dealing and empty entertainment. Hollow to the core, it is the great corporate America write off, a growing rival to the Super Bowl in its commercialism and absence of values. And that's just one of the many reasons why I love it.

It's also a tremendous opportunity for access for journalists, because it's a gathering of the NBA tribes. Star players and rookies, general managers, coaches, retired legends, nameless celebrities — they're all here, waiting to be devoured by a pack of starving, tasteless reporters, more than a thousand of them from all over the world, literally drunk with access, prowling the hotels and bars and press conferences and practices, looking for the next quote. What an ego/power trip. Let's face it. Where else could you shove a microphone or notebook or camera in the face of a rich young superstar, ask obnoxious questions and get away with it?

The weekend got off to an early start last night with a $500 a plate roast for Barkley to raise money for a variety of charities, including Barkley's own scholarship fund and teammate Kevin Johnson's educational program. The emcee was comedian Billy Crystal, who has a new movie, "Forget Paris," about the love life of an NBA referee. (Talk about loveless creatures. Ha!) The film features Barkley among other NBA players.

The night's roasters included teammate Danny Ainge, commissioner David Stern, Phoenix owner Jerry Colangelo and former Suns coach

Cotton Fitzsimmons. Crystal and Ainge, however, ruled the proceedings. Unfortunately, no cameras, microphones, notebooks, etc., were allowed inside, so the media had to work from memory.

"It's easy to roast a guy like Charles who has such an enormous ego," Crystal said, adding that Barkley had no concept of the word "assist."

"Charles is so big, he plays in Phoenix and sh--s in Tucson," Crystal said, warming up the crowd of 1,000. "He weighed 46 pounds at birth. When the doctor slapped him, Charles beat the sh-- out of him."

Crystal pointed out the similarities between Barkley and himself: "He played with Julius Erving. I had two uncles named Julius and Erving."

Crystal also took a few pokes at Ainge. "I asked the waiter for a little white wine," he quipped. "The waiter said, 'Ainge is right over there.'"

He also observed that "Ainge looks so young, he gets fan mail from Michael Jackson."

Ainge, meanwhile, was loaded for Barkley: "He says he's not a role model, but we've seen him naked. We'll put his rolls up against anybody's."

Then he fired off a few new nicknames to replace the old Barkley tag: "Round Mound of Rebound."

How about the "Lard Bard of Right Guard?"

Or, the "Nit Wit of Kid Spit?"

Or, the "MC of No D?"

The event, like the Suns locker room, shed any pretense of political correctness. Reportedly, though, league officials drew the line when Ainge was prepared to bring out a chocolate sculpture of Sir Charles.

In his comments, Barkley noted that he'd been out to dinner with Cleveland Cavaliers coach Mike Fratello about 50 times and had pasta each and every time. "Mike, I am a Negro, and we want chicken and ham hocks," Barkley said.

Sir Charles then called Colangelo and Fitzsimmons "Beavis and Butthead," but later thanked Colangelo for bringing him to Phoenix, adding, "Sooner or later I would have lost one of those bar fights in Philadelphia."

For his foray into these treacherous waters, Stern used a videotape that featured an array of Barkley's antics over the years. The commissioner read his commentary from a prepared script.

"Great job, baby," Crystal said after Stern finished. "Thank you for those spontaneous remarks."

On Friday, the league officially kicked off the weekend with the usual "player availability" session, which allows hundreds of reporters and camera people to wiggle and squirm up close to the two or three best dozen players and coaches in the game for interviews. They were all situated at individual tables inside a massive ballroom at the Pointe Hilton at South Mountain, one of a half dozen resorts the league has booked for the weekend.

This year, the biggest crowd is drawn to Barkley, whom the media have tagged as the weekend's "unofficial host" because he plays for the Suns and Phoenix is hosting the event. Usually a large crowd gathers around Barkley because he always says exactly what he thinks, regardless of what the politics or public relations of the moment might require. His brash sense of humor and an absolute determination to say what he wants when he wants has made Sir Charles a perennial selection on the media's All Interview team. It is also the reason that every NBA insider is certain that Charles will never go into politics. The art of politics involves a fair amount of lying and deception, and Sir Charles is an open book. It's not that he couldn't or wouldn't or hasn't lied. It's usually not his first inclination, however. He'd much rather amuse himself by saying what he thinks.

For example, one of the first questions directed at him this afternoon from the crowd of reporters squeezing around him deals with the 1994 All Star game in Minneapolis, when the Western Conference team went to great lengths to triple team Shaquille O'Neal, then a brilliant and oversized rookie playing in his first All-Star game. Normally, little defense is played on All-Star Weekend and the players have fun "showcasing" their offensive talents. But last year, the Western Conference veterans made an obvious and determined effort to keep O'Neal from dominating.

Barkley blames the media for blowing the situation out of proportion, whatever that might be.

"We wouldn't let him dunk," Barkley tells the reporters around him. "And you all were whining like little bitches afterwards. He's just going by what y'all said."

Such talk, of course, makes the NBA public relations people wince. The league has gone to great efforts to build the All-Star Weekend into an international event, and journalists from dozens of countries — even Cameroon, for example — have come to Phoenix to cover the event, which will be broadcast in about 150 countries worldwide. They've only been here a few hours and already "the unofficial host" is accusing them of whining like little bitches.

The "little bitches," though, obviously love Barkley's antics. With Michael Jordan retired from hoops, the event might be downright boring if not for Mr. Outrageous. Pick any controversial topic and Charles will fire away on it.

Somebody asks him about New Jersey Net badboy Derrick Coleman, who was recently pictured on the cover of Sports Illustrated as an example of the overpaid young players, the X generation crybabies who have come into the league with big fat guaranteed contracts.

"He should be the best player in the league," Barkley says of Coleman, "if he applied hisself more. He hasn't applied hisself. He has more talent in New Jersey than I had in Philadelphia. And in my prime we still were right around .500. That guy, if he played hard, he would be the best player in the league, or one of the top two or three."

"He often compares himself to you," one reporter says, goading Barkley to the next line.

"I play hard all the time," Barkley shoots back. "First of all, he shouldn't compare hisself to me. He should be better. He has more talent than I did in Philadelphia."

Another reporter asks Barkley about the intense competition in the Western Conference between Utah, Phoenix, San Antonio, Seattle and Houston.

"If my back holds up, you don't have to worry about the rest of the conference," Barkley says quickly. "You just have to worry about who we're playing in the Finals."

How is your back? another reporter asks.

"My back is good."

Certainly good enough for Barkley to maintain his absolutely mediocre golf game. The reporters inquire about this morning's showing on the fairways.

"I shot a 38 on the front," Barkley says. "And I pared the last hole, lipped out a birdie putt and had to leave and come down and talk to you cronies. I played great. Only hit one bad shot all day."

Do you kind of feel like the unofficial All Star host? another reporter asks.

"Man, I'm just here to have a good time and to party."

Do you think the Western Conference will win the All-Star game Sunday?

"I don't care about that," Barkley says with a grin. "Winning the All Star game is the least of my worries."

One of his worries is the recent knee injury of Suns forward Danny Manning, who has been lost for the season. Does Manning's injury put more pressure on you, Charles? a reporter asks.

"There was pressure on me anyway," he says. "I have to play well for us to win anyway. Obviously it's going to come down to how my body holds up."

A writer from Seattle asks if Barkley and the Suns are concerned about the Sonics?

"We try not to look behind us," he says, pointing out that Seattle is behind Phoenix in the Pacific Division standings. "We only look straight ahead. We might get hit by a f---ing bus. Y'all are behind us, aren't you? We're not gonna stop to look behind us. We're not gonna turn around."

The other big news in the league is that Houston guard Vernon Maxwell has been fined $20,000 and suspended for 10 games for going up into the stands in Portland and punching a fan. The total loss to Maxwell, including lost salary for games missed, is nearly $300,000. Maxwell says he heard the fan, who was sitting several rows up, making racial slurs and remarks about his deceased infant daughter. Other players and media in the immediate area said they heard no such remarks from the fan.

Barkley, who has been known to take on a fan or two in his day, is asked about the incident.

"I just feel bad," he says. "Even though some fans deserve it, you can't hit them. It's bad. He just can't do that. I feel bad for Vernon."

Next up is a radio reporter from Mexico, who asks, "Mr. Barkley, could you say hello to your fans in Mexico City?"

"Hello my fans in Mexico City," he responds dutifully. "This is Charles Barkley of the Phoenix Suns."

"Tell me something, the growth of the NBA is incredible, no?" the reporter asks. "In Mexico City we have a CBA team and little by little the NBA is growing worldwide."

"Mexican people play basketball?" Barkley asks, faking amazement.

"Yep. We got a CBA team."

"Are there any Mexicans on the team?"

"Nope," the reporter admits.

"All right then," Barkley says. "Self explanatory."

Another reporter points out that former NBA player Greg Grant is on Mexico's CBA team.

"Greg Grant's a good guy," Barkley says, "and I think it's great that the NBA is going to different countries."

"You say that we don't have any Mexicans. . . ," the reporter says in protest.

"I was just joking, man," Barkley says.

"But that's a start, no?" the reporter says. "First we get a CBA franchise, then an NBA franchise."

"I was just joking," Sir Charles repeats. "Joke. Joke. Joke. J-O-K-E."

"Just a last question for Mexico, Charles," the reporter says, asking him to say hello to all the folks south of the border.

Barkley leans into mike and says loudly, "Hello, Mexico, I love you. Keep up the good work, and I hope you win the CBA championship."

The NBA public relations people breathe a sigh of relief. They've just dodged an international incident.

Another noteworthy event on Friday is the practice session for 16-year-old Mike Hoban, a junior varsity player from the suburbs of Cleveland whose name was drawn from six million entries in a Foot Locker shoe store contest. At halftime of Saturday's rookie game, Hoban will get to take one three-point shot, about 22 feet, to win $1 million. If he misses, he still gets $10,000 and the free trip for his family to Phoenix. Foot Locker has tabbed Phoenix guard Dan Majerle to coach Hoban, but in their practice session on Friday, it's obvious that the pressure is building on the kid. He clunks up a series of bricks until he begins making a few.

Majerle, however, shows nothing but confidence. "I'd say he's got about a 40 percent chance of making it," he says. "I like his form. He does the same things over and over again and has good motion. All he has to do is just relax and shoot it."

Relaxing is the hard part, of course, for a 16-year-old facing a giant moment in his life. Make the shot and his family is set. Miss it, well, and spend the rest of your life thinking about what might have been. It seems like a heavy burden just so Foot Locker can get all of that free promotional attention.

"Right now I feel great about it," Hoban says, not sounding real convinced. "I've spent a lot of time out in the driveway."

Hoban's big shot is just one of dozens of gigs scheduled for All Star Weekend. Up until the last minute, the NBA's promoters were busy arranging the appearances of entertainers and non-sports celebrities. In recent years, they've snared the likes of rapper Hammer, vocal group Boyz II Men, TV star Jaleel White and baseball Hall of Famer Reggie Jackson.

Even civil rights activist Jesse Jackson found a courtside seat at last year's event in Minneapolis.

This year, the big names are Bill Cosby, the Four Tops and Kenny Rogers. Oh well.

The league's main effort is focused on hyping and promoting its young players. Shaq, Anfernee Hardaway, Grant Hill, Chris Webber, Latrell Sprewell, and several dozen others will be on hand to strike stars in the eyes of fans. There is still room, however, for the game's all-time greats. Although the league has dropped its Legends game in favor of a Legends long-distance shooting competition, the old timers still view the All Star game as a place to hang out. "This weekend is basically a reunion, and a warm one," said Hall of Famer Dave Bing, one of many legends who gather in a separate hotel to reminisce about the NBA's gritty days. The league that they knew bears little resemblance to the modern corporate approach to pro basketball as entertainment.

Two years ago, the league added Fleer's NBA Jam Session to the schedule. It's an interactive, multifaceted basketball carnival that is open much of the weekend and includes a variety of games and three-on-three competitions for fans, autograph sessions, displays by card and equipment manufacturers and even a card and memorabilia show. By NBA standards, admission to the Jam Session is relatively cheap (about $10), although the league and Phoenix area businesses will be busy handing out numerous passes and discounts.

All of this extracurricular fun occurs in conjunction with the weekend's schedule of All-Star events — the rookie game, the legends shootout, the long-distance shootout, slam dunk competition and the All-Star game itself.

The weekend opens with a "Meet The Stars" Jam Session on Friday night, then shifts to the All-Star Stay In School Celebration on Saturday morning, where local school students with perfect attendance are given a commemorative card sheet and a reserved seat to see the stars introduced.

Saturday afternoon and evening bring the rookie game, long-distance shootout and slam-dunk competition, and Sunday evening is the All-Star Game itself, which will be broadcast worldwide.

The breadth of the schedule itself stands in stark contrast to the atmosphere in 1951 when Boston Celtics owner Walter Brown came up with the idea of holding a midseason all-star game. At the time, basketball was struggling to overcome the black eye left by a series of college gambling scandals in 1950. "Even up until the last week, the game was in doubt," Brown once recalled. "A few days before the game, Maurice Podoloff, the commissioner, called me on the phone and asked me to call it off. He said that everyone he talked to said it would be a flop, and that the league would look bad."

Only Brown's determination allowed the game to survive through the NBA's lean seasons. But the sport grew, and over the years innovation came from unlikely places.

In 1976, the rival American Basketball Association came along and instituted a slam dunk competition at its All-Star event, and the 17,798 fans in Denver's brand new McNichols Arena went nuts. David Thompson battled Julius Erving in that first legendary showdown staged at halftime of the ABA All-Star game.

Erving prevailed, and the idea of basketball as entertainment was firmly ensconced in the mind's of NBA promoters. By 1984, the league had developed the game into the All-Star Weekend, the format from which the modern show has exploded. Magic Johnson's last big NBA appearance came at the 1992 Weekend in Orlando in what many consider the All Star game's greatest and most emotional moment, when the HIV-positive Johnson was named the MVP.

Now, regardless of the lack of substance, there's no question that the entire basketball world looks forward to each Weekend with great anticipation. "It's a great show," says Phoenix coach Paul Westphal. "It's been compared to the Super Bowl, and in a lot of ways it's more appropriate to have this kind of spectacle in an All Star game than in a championship game. So I think it's a forum to showcase the NBA, and it's a pleasure to be a part of it."

"The excitement is here," agrees David Robinson. "It just seems like every year the pageantry around it gets a little bigger, the hype gets a little bigger."

This has been particularly true in Phoenix, a basketball-crazy town if there ever was one. The population has gone nuts over hoops, and frankly, the NBA has found itself being overrun by crowds it never anticipated. Last year in frosty Minneapolis, the events were often deserted, resembling a mausoleum. But hundreds of thousands of people have crammed into downtown Phoenix, all of them seeking to reach out and touch the real live NBA. As with most modern versions of the All Star game, this one has brightly colored banners hanging everywhere, and high prices on every item loose enough to sell. Anything that's got a little Suns' orange and purple and a splash of gold on it is bringing at least 15 bucks. The choke of humanity in the NBA Jam Session last night was oppressive. Lines for the events were longer than Disneyworld. Every step had to be calculated. It was a constant duck and weave and bob through the crowds, a suffocating atmosphere.

Saturday morning brings even greater crowds because the All Stars are scheduled to appear at the Jam Session in the Phoenix Civic Plaza to hold practice. By mid morning, the building is crammed and security guards are turning thousands of people away, creating a series of angry scenes with frustrated fans.

Those lucky enough to get inside find the Eastern Conference team practicing first. Actually, it's not so much a practice as it is a preening session, with players dunking for the crowds. The Eastern coach, Orlando's Brian Hill, recognized the impossibility of the situation. "You're gonna do what you're gonna do," he tells his players, "but we want to try and add a little organization anyway."

Moments later, Shaq slams, and the fans go wild.

The session lasts an hour, then the Western Conference squad appears on the floor, and suddenly the arena is awash in media and camera crews as players and coaches from both teams spend 30 minutes giving impromptu interviews.

The most notable absence on the Western squad is Rodman, who was not picked as an All Star despite the fact that he is well on his way to claiming a fourth straight league rebounding title, a feat that only Wilt Chamberlain and Moses Malone have accomplished. Deeply wounded at the snub, Rodman responded by pointing out that "the All Star Game is for politicians to get together and eat steak and lobster. You put makeup on these people and all of a sudden what have you got? You've got Mary Kay selling cosmetics on the hardwood in Phoenix. They don't want Dennis Rodman anywhere near something that good. They don't like the way I am. . . being a real human being playing a fiction game.

"I would make the game exciting," Rodman said. "People would be on the edge of their seats wondering what I was going to do."

Instead of entertaining in Phoenix, Rodman spent the weekend in Vegas, rolling bones.

"I didn't talk to him too much," David Robinson says when asked about Rodman. "but I let him know, 'Hey, I felt like he should have been here.' He's played great. He's been the best rebounder in the league by far. He's been fantastic. It's been disappointing that he didn't make it, but there's a lot of guys who should have made it and didn't so there's not a lot you can say.

"With Dennis, we're a completely different team," Robinson said of the Spurs. "We have confidence and power in different ways that other teams just don't have. I have no doubt that we can win the West with Dennis in the right frame of mind the rest of the year."

A few feet away, Barkley is holding court as the media swirl around him, the kleig lights casting him in a surreal glare, the motor drives humming, the tape machines rolling.

"Is there anything about playing the Knicks that particularly gets your blood boiling?" a New York writer asks.

"No," Barkley says tersely.

Undaunted, the writer persists: "When you think of the Knicks what do you think of?"

"A very physical team. They just work hard. I don't think they're really that talented. I think they work very hard to make up for that lack of talent. And if the refs let 'em cheat, they'll win. If they don't let 'em cheat, I don't think they'll win."

"Do you expect to see them in the Finals?" the writer asks.

"I don't know," Barkley says, "but it depends. If the refs let 'em play that style they play, they got a chance to win it. But if the game is the way it's supposed to be played, the way the new rules say it's supposed to be played, they don't have a chance."

The writer smiles at this. "You think they cheat a little bit?" he asks.

"I know they cheat," Barkley says. "The league had to change the rules because of them. They didn't do it for no other reason. "

The writer suggests that Barkley's opinion is controversial.

"That's not controversial," Barkley shoots back. "Just because somebody says something you don't agree with, that doesn't make it controversial. That's another example of the media right there. If someone voices an opinion different from yours, that doesn't make it controversial. That's how the media works. Their job is to get us boiling mad at each other."

Sensing that Charles is about to overheat, the reporter mumbles, "Thanks," and moves on. Somebody else inquires about his golf game again.

"I'm playing really well on the golf course as you know," he says. "I played even better yesterday. I only missed one fairway."

Another reporter asks if Charles sees himself as one of the few high-profile guys left in the game now that Michael's retired.

"The game will always be fine," he says. "There will always be great players coming on the horizon."

From the edge of the crowd, an ESPN reporter squeezes in and says, "Charles, we're doing a series on groupies in the NBA. Is it as bad as everyone says it is?"

"No," Barkley says. "That's another media misconception. Everybody talks about groupies this and that. Number one, they should get a life. I mean the media. Number two, any guy out there in society who is handsome and has got a lot of money, women are going to try to talk to him, so the groupie thing is a sick subject, and you guys should get a f---in' life."

"Thank you," the ESPN reporter says and starts to move away.

"Motherf----r," Barkley says, turning back to the reporters standing around him. "See, that's why I hate white people."

Moving right along, a Canadian news team steps up in front of him. "We're from Vancouver," the reporter says. "How do you feel about traveling to Vancouver and Tornanto next year with expansion?"

"I don't like expansion. It just waters the league down, and they're just bad teams."

"So you're not the least bit happy about the situation?"

"Not really happy," Barkley repeats. "I think expansion in sports is not a good idea because the league is watered down enough. Obviously teams are not going to do well. They're going to make money, but that's not the most important thing. I like to see good basketball teams."

"What about long term?" the Canadian asks. "Expansion takes the game to other countries around the world."

"I'm not concerned about that," Barkley says. "I just like seeing good basketball."

"You don't really hate white people," says another reporter standing nearby, grinning at Barkley.

"I'm just f---ing wit you," he says.

"I know," the reporter says.

Someone else asks about the city of Phoenix.

"I'm in a very lucky situation," Barkley says. "We have a great team in Phoenix, a great arena, great fans. This is a great city to live in. I'm just fortunate to be a part of it."

Suddenly a German TV crew steps up. "You still enjoy all the bustle around you, huh, Charles?" the reporter asks.

"Man, you just have to deal with all these people. You enjoy, but you have to deal with it. It goes with the territory."

"So the media is wondering, vat vill Charles Barkley do after they retire his jersey?"

"I don't worry too much about the future. I think it's just important to enjoy your life while it's happening."

"What about his politician thing? Governor?" the German asks.

"That will happen in a few years hopefully," Barkley says. "But if it doesn't, it'll be all right. I just want to enjoy myself, and that makes my life good."

"So do you know Helmut Kohl, the German chancellor?" the reporter asks.

"I know his name," Barkley says. "I don't know him personally."

"He is as big as you are," the German says, "but he isn't as mobile."

"His job is probably more significant than mine, though," Charles concedes. "His job is a lot more important than mine."

The swirl of news teams is almost dizzying now. Following the Germans is a pretty blonde reporter. "Mr. Barkley, are you gonna be governor of Alabama?" she asks.

"I hope to be."

"Do you have a first lady?"

"I sure do."

"Oh," the reporter says, the disappointment tangible in her voice. "Well, see you out on the golf course."

Barkley shakes his head as she moves away. Somebody else asks him about his platform as governor.

"Man, give me a break," he says. "Don't make me think today."

The questions, though, keep coming fast and furiously. BET wants to know if he is a statesman for black America. Others want to know what he thinks of the baseball strike.

Suddenly a Nickelodeon crew looms in front of him. "You came up on our top 10 list with all the kids," the Nickelodeon reporter says.

"I got a plaque and that was really nice," Barkley says. "It meant a great deal to me. Kids are the best part of my job, and that meant a lot to me."

They briefly discuss the Stay-In-School Program held that morning for area school children. Then Nickelodeon propositions Charles Barkley to do a promo.

"Our show is called Bing," the reporter explains.

"Bing???" Barkley asks.

"As in Butta Bing," the reporter says. "The sound is something new. All the kids wrote in and wanted to know what sound effect is Charles Barkley. If you were a sound effect, go for it. What sound would you be?"

"I don't know what kind of sound I'd be, man."

"A big sound or a little sound, how 'bout that?" the reporter says.

"I would probably be a little sound," Barkley says. "Just a little sound."

"Okay, cool. And how about your favorite slam dunk?"

"My favorite?"

"That you do."

"Oh, I can't dunk anymore."

"What did I do?" the reporter asks. "Step on your foot?"

"No, I'm not near as good as I used to be," Barkley says with a chuckle.

Through the crowd of reporters comes 90-year-old Les Harrison, the feisty former owner of the old Rochester Royals. He's one of the NBA's pioneering owners, yet here he is, wanting Charles Barkley's autograph. It's for a friend, he says. But that's what they all say.

Unfortunately, Les has a hard time being heard over the crowd in the arena, which is thundering a chant. Barklee! Barklee! Barklee! They just want him to wave. There's a lady. She must be 40. A blonde on the front row, leaning over the railing, waving at any reporter's eye she can catch, screaming, "I'm his number one fan. Please get him to turn around and wave!"

Finally Barkley turns and waves. And the crowd responds like some phototropic organism, some giant amoeba or something, thousands of arms are fluttering, vocal chords are vibrating in excitement, in worship of Charles Barkley, leaving me thinking that humans are more than a bit strange.

Charles must be thinking the same thing, because he turns to an NBA public relations staffer standing nearby. "Can we get these cronies outta here?" Barkley shouts, motioning to the reporters around him.

Standing patiently nearby is 90-year-old Les Harrison, still hoping for the autograph.

"I got to get him to sign this," Harrison tells me, then turns to Barkley and says, "I want you to sign this."

Someone explains to Barkley that Harrison is the former owner/coach of the Royals, that they won the league title in 1951 with a flashy superstar guard named Bob Davies, while Harrison ranted and raved at the officials from the bench. In his day, Les Harrison was every bit as mouthy and eccentric as Charles Barkley.

Sir Charles pauses and signs for Harrison.

"Thank you," the old man says.

"You're very welcome, sir," Barkley responds.

Someone else asks him to sign something for Becky.

"C'mon now," Charles says with a grin. "I don't know Becky."

Sadly, the All Star Weekend goes downhill from there. That afternoon, Mike Hoban gets a chance at his million-dollar shot. He shoots an airball.

This, of course, is devastating, his being only 16 and all, and an airball being a profound embarrassment. The next day, I'm on a media courtesy bus headed to the All-Star Game, and I notice that Hoban is sitting alone in the seat in front of me, obviously lost in a very dark mood, staring morosely out the window. I sure hope Foot Locker enjoyed its promotion. Just maybe it would be a good idea for corporate America not to prey on minors when it needs somebody to play the fool in one of its nationally televised promotions. Just maybe it would be better if they had an old fart like me missing the million dollar shots. It certainly would be much better if an old fart like me made one.

On television this morning, ESPN was running a news clip of Charles Barkley saying that he hates white people. Although Sir Charles was obviously intending the remark as a humorous aside, ESPN thinks that just maybe it has the spark of controversy. Barkley is forced to respond that he in no way hates white people (he's even married to one). "In the press you're always going to have a few idiots who want controversy or want to make things bad," he says. "That's the unfortunate part of our sports. What happens is, the press has so much control, people will start believing that. That's the main problem I have with the press, the general population will believe what they read or what they hear on the radio, even if it has no basis in fact, or it's not good at all. If I do an interview, I'll talk to somebody for five minutes, and they'll put three seconds of it on the sound bite. Any time you show that, it can always be manipulated."

On Sunday evening, the Western Conference All Stars badly outclass the Eastern Conference. In the waning moments of the game, Shaquille O'Neal takes a rare three-pointer and misses very badly. I hope Mike Hoban saw that one, I think, as the arena fills with chants of "Air-Ball!"

"Oh, my goodness," David Robinson later says of Shaq's trey. "He better work on that one. That was about four feet short. I'm sure he shoots it better than that in practice."

After the game, a group of reporters crowds around Barkley's locker. It contains three pictures of his little girl and a poster that says, "That which does not kill me only makes me stronger." In addition, there is a golf hat, his deck shoes, and a note some little girl has written professing love.

When he walks up, I say mischievously, "I wanted to ask you a question about groupies."

He eyes me cautiously. "You again?"

I tell him I'm just kidding, that I wasn't the one who asked that question yesterday. But it's too late.

"I tell you what," he says. "I'm gonna go sit in the steam room and whirl pool and drink a couple of beers. Then I'm gonna come back and deal with you all."

"Can I ask you a couple of question about the game?" another reporter asks.

"Naw, man," Sir Charles says. "I'm gonna go sit in the whirlpool. Talk to these other guys. They were sh-- players. I don't want to play with them. I need some real players. I need Manute Bol."

At this, he walks off with a large Ha! Ha! Ha! echoing through the locker room. Once again, it seems that Sir Charles, the ambassador of Phoenix, has found a way to laugh the last laugh.

CHICAGO HOPE
THE UNITED CENTER — MARCH 1995

The ritual begins each game night with the house lights going black and the tape deck kicking in, hammering out those familiar Alan Parsons Project chords, the heavy, synthesized, eerie ones that sound like the score for some science fiction horror flick. You know, like Alien III is on the premises or something.

Simultaneously, lines of green laser lights begin gyrating wildly and raking across the audience, mesmerizing yet another sellout of 21,711. All the while the spotlight focuses on the giant Bulls face, the team logo, at center court, and soon the laser lights stop their dancing and fall to the arena floor to reshape themselves into giant green Bulls heads.

The problem is, if you watch these lights too closely you risk missing the main show on the scoreboard's massive videoscreens overhead. They, too, fill with the angry visage of a Bull, a computer-designed, nineties kind of animal, who turns and snorts his way through the city's canyons, pausing along the way to scare the bejiggers out of a bronze lion in front of the Art Institute.

From there, the Bull elevates his game on some sort of vacuum-cushioned hooves and whisks his way up and down the streets, like a tourist lost in traffic, looking for that renowned Madison Street. You might even say that he passes some familiar landmarks, except this urban environment is sterile and clean and crisp as a laser print and hauntingly unfamiliar.

Heck, when the Bull finally does locate Madison and storms his way out to the United Center, he finds the building set in a vast, green meadow. To make sure you get the picture, the artist rotates the view of the building as the Bull searches for the press gate. Sure enough, it's green meadows all around, as if hundreds of urban blocks have been plowed under and reseeded.

Just as you're beginning to contemplate the implications of all this, public address announcer Ray Clay brings you back to the business at hand with his patented, deeply etched introduction, 'AND NOW, YOUR CHICAGO BULLS!!!'

On cue, the crowd pushes the decibel level another notch toward infinity, and just in case there's a need for any extra noise, the United Center's architects have placed sound reflectors in the ceiling, which knock the waves back to the arena floor. To say the least, it is oppressive, which makes the players on opposing teams thankful that the lights are down. Otherwise, the home fans might be able to see just how distracted and unsettled they are by this display.

The introduction of each of the Bulls' starting five gooses the crowd a bit higher, and by the time Ray Clay works around to calling out Scottie Pippen's name, the sound in the building has built to a heavy metal quality, one in which the particles are being shoved around so forcefully that the air seems momentarily transformed from gas to solid.

Solid noise. And it hurts.

Then the fireworks in the rafters go off, raining sparks and light and smoke down on 21,711 heads until finally it's over, except for the emergency recovery work going on in your ears.

It didn't used to be this way, of course. Back in the old days, you got your beer and popcorn and your basic four quarters of hoop. Promotions were something employees got if they did a good job.

In 1966, when the Bulls were a new team and attempting to celebrate their first season with a parade, they could muster just two flatbed trucks for the procession — one for the staff and one for a frightened bull they had arranged to borrow for the afternoon from the nearby stockyards, a sight that left local reporters shaking their heads in amusement.

Yes, it seems the Bulls have come a long way in 30 years.

On the other hand, they've merely moved across the street, from one side of the 1900 block of West Madison to the other.

Here, inside the United Center, is the future of pro hoops, but outside, just north across Madison, is the game's past, the remains of Chicago Stadium. In the dusk of this Wednesday night in March, the Stadium stands as silent and eerie as a graveyard. Over the coming months, demolition crews will persistently digest the grand old "sandstone sarcophagus," eating away first at the insides, then attacking the shell, until only the steel framework and neat piles of rubble remain.

Tonight, the old building stands with a gigantic hole knocked in its west wall, revealing that the interior is still largely intact. For the ticket holders arriving for tonight's game, it is unsettling to see the giant wound in this landmark. Even stranger, the lights are on inside, as if the spirits of games past are anxiously awaiting the crowd's arrival for another tipoff.

Just months ago, the buildings' circumstances were reversed. Then, the United Center was a framework under construction, standing silently, while the Stadium, the "Madhouse on Madison," thundered with the exhortations of some 18,676 fans. Tonight, though, the only sound in the Stadium is the relentless Chicago wind pushing through the vast hole and rattling the lights. Soon the Stadium will fade altogether, into a parking lot.

Sometimes during his workday, Tim Hallam, the Bulls director of media services, retreats from his spacious new office in the United Center to the sidewalk outside, for a smoke. These retreats are a bit uncomfortable these days because Hallam, who has worked games at the Stadium for 17 years, doesn't like looking at the grand old building in its hour of demise. He couldn't quite bring himself to gather with the crowd that witnessed the wrecking ball first striking the west wall just days ago. "It was a little bit of a funeral," he explained.

Even Bulls' chairman Jerry Reinsdorf, the man who built the United Center with Blackhawks chairman Bill Wirtz, admits to being unsettled by the sight of the Stadium going down. "But it's just a building," he says. "It needed to be replaced. What's important are the memories of what happened there, and the memories will live for a long, long time."

Research suggests that the senses drive the memory, so the Stadium is destined like her sister building, Boston Garden — which also is scheduled for razing in the coming months — to be remembered for the peculiar smells of old arenas, decades of stale popcorn and spilled beer and sweat.

Pungent as these were, the overriding sensory impact of the Stadium was the noise itself, which helps explain why the team has gone out of its way to make sure the United Center is just as deafening. "There was no place like Chicago Stadium," says former Bulls general manager Rod Thorn, now an NBA executive. "The acoustics in that old building just drove the noise down right over the floor, and it just hovered there. It made it impossible to hear anything."

Everyone, it seems, has a favorite recollection of this impossibility. When was it the loudest? For many, that date is May 1989, Game 6 of the Eastern Conference Finals, the Bulls vs. the Detroit Pistons. Toward the end of the third quarter, Pistons center Bill Laimbeer, that dastardly villain, stepped to the free throw line, and somehow the same thought was instantly and magically transmitted into the minds of the 18,676 people in attendance.

"Laim-beer sucks! Laim-beer sucks! Laim-beer sucks!" they intoned over and over until, sadly, he canned both shots.

Kip Motta, son of former Bulls coach Dick Motta, likes to think of the 1974 playoffs when he was a young ball boy and the Bulls were facing the Pistons at home for Game 7 of their playoff battle. Jerry Sloan, the team's gutsy leader, had been injured in Game 6 in Detroit and was unable to play. "We were warming up," Motta recalled, "and you could tell there was no excitement. It was like a cloud of doom over us because Jerry wasn't gonna play. But when he came up out of the locker room on his crutches, the crowd gave him a standing ovation. It was the loudest, most intense ovation I've ever heard. It was unbelievable. They went crazy. For four or five minutes, they didn't stop. And it got louder and louder all the time."

Buoyed by the fan support, the Bulls pulled together and beat Detroit to win the series.

"I was reluctant to even go up there," Sloan remembered recently. "But I wanted to watch the game."

Now the coach of the Utah Jazz, Sloan's fondest Chicago memories are of the Stadium. "I spent a great deal of my life in basketball in that building," he said, "and it was one of the greatest places if you were a player. Having the fan support in that building to me was the height of excitement. The playoff games that we had, even though you remember the losses, the games that we played in there and the games that we won, the feeling was incredible.

"These days people talk about noisy buildings, but a lot of that is electronic, manufactured noise. There wasn't much going on back in the Stadium except people yelling and raising hell every time they came out to the game. If they came, they came to yell. They didn't come to see who was gonna look at them and see what they looked like. There wasn't very many people sitting there in mink coats, either. It was hard core fans.

"And they'd boo your ass, too, if you didn't play well," Sloan remembered with a grin. "We were getting beat one night against New York. The Knicks had us down 28 points at half time, and our fans booed us off the floor. We responded to it. We came right back out in the second half and beat the Knicks, and that's when New York was good, when they had Willis Reed and Walt Frazier and that bunch."

"The loudest I ever heard it," says Hallam, "was when Jerry Sloan was coaching and we were playing the Knicks in the best-of-three miniseries in the first round of the 1981 playoffs and we went to overtime.

"That was back when people were smoking in the upper balconies and you had the haze hanging over the floor. That's why it was such a great — I don't want to say it — but a great 'sixth man.' It was so loud it was crazy. You weren't exactly fearful, but you could tell that anything could happen. It was very intimidating for officials, for visiting teams, because it looked like all hell could break loose at any time."

Standing here at dusk, you can almost hear the echoes of these and a thousand other events, Blackhawks Stanley Cup victories, prizefights, ice shows, Globetrotter comedy hours, even an NFL game or two. Michael Jordan made his final playing appearance in the Stadium last year, at a charity game hosted by Scottie Pippen. On departing at the end of the game, Jordan got down and kissed the floor, the very platform of his rise to greatness. It was the only sendoff the Madhouse really needed.

Now, these two buildings are passing in the night. How strange. How appropriate. Perhaps Reinsdorf is right. History isn't special until something changes or someone dies. Tonight the Stadium is dying, but its history lives.

Across the street, as the Bulls prepare to tipoff against the Atlanta Hawks, the fans find themselves quite comfortable in Reinsdorf's grand vision of the future. While the United Center may not cater to their every whim, it comes close, offering a basketball carnival of live bands, interactive games and an array of food and drink.

On this Wednesday night in March, this party atmosphere courses with a new electricity, and the fans have their thoughts turned to the past, not to the Stadium, but to the rumored return of Michael Jordan to basketball.

To them, the Jordan story is as familiar as their own. You, too, may have heard of him. He's the shooting guard who led the Bulls to their days of glory, or more specifically to three straight NBA championships. Remember his flash dance to the basket during the 1991 victory over the Los Angeles Lakers and Magic Johnson? And how about his matter-of-fact shrug after hitting all those threes to dash Clyde Drexler and the

Portland Trail Blazers for the 1992 title? Or the way he toyed with the New York Knicks and the Phoenix Suns in '93?

The fans had been a part of all of it, a big part. Jordan had said as much many times over, and for that he had thanked them just a few months ago, on November 1, 1994, the night his jersey number 23 was retired and his statue was unveiled outside the United Center.

Perhaps the most special moment came in 1992 after their second championship. The Bulls had vanquished Portland in Game 6, and after the game the players retreated to the locker room to engage in the usual ritual, spewing their champagne, wearing their new hats backwards, doing their media interviews and hugging lots of hugs.

And the fans, as usual, were supposed to go away, to file out the aisles of the Stadium and retreat to their cars to face the post-game traffic. Only this time they didn't want to turn the moment loose. So they stayed, thundering on in celebration. A curtain call for a basketball team? Unheard of.

Still they thundered. So the players and coaches trudged back up the steep, narrow stairs from the bowels of the Stadium and cast themselves into the center of an unprecedented lovefest.

"We went down to the locker room for the presentation of the trophy," Jerry Reinsdorf recalled. "We must have been down there close to half an hour when somebody mentioned the crowd hadn't left. The team went back up on the floor, and the players got up on the scorer's table and started dancing and holding the trophy up for the fans. The crowd just yelled and yelled and yelled. It was a wonderful, exhilarating feeling.

"I've never seen so much love pouring out from a crowd."

It was a transcendent moment, and now Bulls fans understandably want more of them, want Michael to end his 18-month "retirement" from basketball so they can all share in more glory, more special feelings.

Even though it won't come on this night against the Atlanta Hawks, Jordan's impending return has created a noticeable lift in spirits here. During the 1993-94 season, the first without Jordan, the Bulls accomplished incredible things. They stacked up 55 wins and battled their way to the Eastern Conference Finals yet again, only to lose Game 5 to New York on a controversial, last-second call that helped cost them the series.

But this season, the team has struggled to stay above .500, leaving frustration and some despair, a sense that the Bulls' — and to some degree the city's — hour of greatness is slipping away, much like the Stadium across the street is slipping into darkness.

Only now, the rumor of Michael's return has evaporated those anxieties and replaced them with golden thoughts. There's no better evidence of this than the recent boom in retail business in Bulls memorabilia, in jerseys and hats and T-shirts and coffee mugs, anything sporting the team's logo or Jordan's No. 23.

"This is all about hope," observes Brad Riggert, manager of Fandemonium, the United Center's fan store, after watching thousands of shoppers plucking items from the shelves in recent days. "Michael's return is bringing back hope to the fans, hope to the whole city."

Hope, indeed. For decades, that has been the fuel driving Chicago basketball. At times it ran high. More often it ebbed low. In the early 1970s, when Jerry Sloan and Norm Van Lier and Chet Walker and Bob Love and Tom Boerwinkle shoved their way to NBA respect, the hope was based on their work ethic, that good old hogbutcher, stacker-of-wheat, city-of-big-shoulders mentality. They were desperate Bulls, willing to sacrifice their health to be winners.

Jordan, of course, was none of that. Instead, he brought the hope of flight, of a special magic, of new possibilities, of glass box buildings and laser lights. His talent has built this phantasmagoria of success, the United Center, and it seems only right that he should play here, in this new age of pro basketball that he has helped to create.

That, above all, is on the fans' minds this Wednesday night in March of 1995. The special feelings are abundant. The fans know that hope is back. Bigger than ever. And, once again, it has wings.

For 10 days, it has been the greatest tease in the history of sport. Was Michael Jordan returning to basketball or not? From Warsaw to Waukegan, the planet clamored to know.

Finally on Saturday, March 18, 1995, he broke his silence with a two-word press release, issued through agent David Falk.

I'm back.

Sure enough, the next day, shortly after noon, he emerged with his teammates from the visitors' locker room at Market Square Arena in Indianapolis, where the Bulls were scheduled to meet the Indiana Pacers.

Standing before the crowd gathered in the hallway outside the locker room was Superman himself, chomping his gum fiercely. The greatest basketball player in the history of the game was ready to resume the career that had been interrupted by an 18-month 'retirement.'

Instamatics flashed, and people wiggled with excitement. "This is just like the President appearing," commented one Chicago TV reporter.

"Are you kidding?" somebody else said. "Michael's more important than that."

Only now, just as he was raring to take the floor and restart his career, something was wrong. Jordan's face tightened. Somebody was missing.

The Bulls did a quick head count. Only eleven. "Who's not here?" Jordan asked as he searched the faces around him.

They all turned to see Scottie Pippen sheepishly slipping out of the locker room.

With his jaws working the gum and his glare policing the roster, Jordan gathered his teammates in a huddle, where they joined hands.

"What time is it?" forward Corie Blount yelled.

"It's game time!" they answered in unison.

With that, the Bulls broke and made their way out into the arena, opening the latest chapter in the strange, wonderful saga of Air Jordan.

Michael was back, and the news flashed around the world. Everywhere, it seemed, fans were reassuring themselves that basketball's heart was once again beating, that the sport they loved no longer needed life support.

"He is like a gift from God to the basketball game," Huang Gang, a 21-year-old professional player in Beijing, remarked upon hearing the news. "We try to imitate his ground moves. But you can't copy him in the air. He is unique."

Waiting for the competition to begin that Sunday in Indianapolis, Pacers coach Larry Brown quipped that the atmosphere was so zany, it seemed like "Elvis and the Beatles are back."

The proceedings did have a dreamlike feel about them. But that's how we define superstars, isn't it? By their ability to suspend reality? Jordan had always done that for Bulls fans. Yet the circumstances were never more ethereal than 10 days ago, when the first rumors leaked out that he was contemplating another career move.

Without question, the Bulls were caught off guard by Jordan's decision to abandon the professional baseball career he had launched upon leaving basketball. Many people in baseball had questioned his skill level after he immersed himself in the White Sox minor league farm system, but no one doubted his work ethic. In his determination to learn to hit big league pitching, Jordan came early and stayed late each day at practice.

But the futility was obvious almost from the start. He was too tall, some said, and presented too big a strike zone. "He is attempting to compete with hitters who have seen 350,000 fastballs in their baseball lives and 204,000 breaking balls,'" Rangers pitching instructor Tom House appraised shortly after Jordan joined the AA Birmingham Barons for the 1994 season. "Baseball is a function of repetition. If Michael had pursued baseball out of high school, I don't doubt he would have wound up making as much money in baseball as in basketball. But he's not exactly tearing up Double A, and that's light years from the big leagues."

If he was light years away, Jordan, a 32-year-old .200 hitter, certainly didn't have time to waste with the protracted baseball strike that had loomed over the game for eight months. Hoping it would soon be resolved, he reported to spring training in Florida only to realize that the fight between owners and players over money wasn't going to end anytime soon. Then, he had a misunderstanding with White Sox management over dressing room and parking arrangements. So he packed up and went home.

Within days of his departure from Florida, a Chicago radio station reported that Jordan was secretly working out with the Bulls and contemplating a return to basketball.

On March 10, he announced his retirement from baseball, saying his minor league experience had been powerful because it allowed him to rediscover the work ethic that had made him a great basketball player. "I met thousands of new fans," he said, "and I learned that minor league players are really the foundation of baseball. They often play in obscurity and with little recognition, but they deserve the respect of the fans and everyone associated with the game."

Michael Jordan hadn't failed baseball, Phil Jackson noted. "Baseball failed him."

Soon the Bulls confirmed that Jordan was working out with the team, and Jackson revealed that Jordan had actually been contemplating a return since October.

Like that, the situation exploded. Scores of media representatives from the major networks and national publications converged on the Berto Center, the Bulls' practice facility in suburban Deerfield, in anticipation of Michael holding a press conference announcing his return.

Yet each day at practice, large screens covered the picture windows through which reporters observed Bulls practices. The media could hear the shouts, the squeaking of sneakers on the gym floor. They were told that Michael was practicing with the team but that he hadn't yet made up his mind about returning, that the details were being worked out.

On the Berto Center floor, Michael displayed the intense competitiveness that for years had charged Bulls' practice sessions.

Wearing the yellow vest of the second team, he ran point guard against the regulars and reminded them just what true greatness meant. "Just to be able to play with him is fun," said center Will Perdue. "Just to be able to watch him."

Still, Jordan wavered that week, pausing, as he would later explain, to contemplate whether he was returning to basketball out of disappointment over the baseball strike, or if he was in fact returning because he loved the game. This self-evaluation came at the urging of Jerry Reinsdorf, who didn't want Jordan to leave the game only to regret it later. While the media speculated and fans kept the lines buzzing on sports radio talk shows, Jordan remained silent. The closest he came to making a statement was the revving of his burgundy Corvette, warning the media to get out of the roadway as he left practice each day.

His silence drove reporters and fans alike to distraction, with some callers on Chicago's sports radio talk shows claiming that Jordan was toying with the public.

Meanwhile, USA Today reported that the stock value of companies who employed Jordan as a spokesman had zoomed up $2 billion on the various stock exchanges in recent days, leading to further speculation that Jordan was engaged in some kind of financial manipulation.

Finally, on Thursday March 16, Jackson told Jordan not to attend practice that day because the media crowd at the Berto Center had gotten too large. After practice, Jackson revealed to a swarm of reporters that Jordan and Reinsdorf were engaged in discussions and that a decision was three or four days away.

That Friday night, the Bulls capped a three-game winning streak and raised their record three notches above .500 by defeating the Milwaukee Bucks in the United Center. Speculation had been high that Jordan might make a sudden appearance in uniform for that game, but only his security advisers showed up to evaluate the arena.

Early the next morning, the Chicago radio waves were abuzz that Jordan would make his announcement that day, and that he would play Sunday in the nationally televised game against Indiana. Down on LaSalle Street, the managers at Michael Jordan's Restaurant heard the news and decided that they better restock the gift shop yet again. The restaurant's business had been slow in February, but the hint of Jordan's return had turned March into a boom, with crowds packing the place virtually every night.

As a result, the gift shop was doing a whopping business, selling miniature bats, trading cards, jerseys, posters, coffee mugs and other trinkets. Other fans gathered at the Jordan statue outside the United Center. Revealed in a nationally televised retirement ceremony in November, the statue had quickly become a hot spot for fans and tourists in Chicago. On this Saturday, as the anticipation grew, small groups were drawn to the statue.

"This is like the Colts returning to Baltimore," said one fan, "with Johnny Unitas as quarterback!"

Over at the Berto Center in Deerfield, crowds of fans and reporters milled about, with many fans hanging from the balconies and walls of the Residence Inn next door. Nine different TV satellite trucks hovered near the building, waiting to blast the news around the world.

Suddenly, practice was over, and like that, Jordan's burgundy 'Vette appeared on the roadway, with him gunning his engine and the fans cheering wildly as he sped off. Next came Pippen in a Range Rover, pausing long enough to flash a giant smile through the vehicle's darkly tinted windows.

Moments later, NBC's Peter Vescey did a stand up report outside with the fans rooting in the background. He told the broadcast audience that Jordan was returning, that Jordan would play against Indiana on Sunday and probably wear his old number 23, which had been retired in November. The excitement coursed through the city. Chicago, quipped one radio sportscaster, was in a state of 'Jorgasym.'

Jordan did not fly to Indianapolis with the team that Saturday night. A crowd of fans and media gathered at the Canterbury Hotel, awaiting the Bulls' arrival. When a limousine with a police escort pulled up, the crowd surged forward. But out stepped a bride and groom. "Who are these people?" the stunned bride asked her new husband.

The team showed up moments later and was roundly cheered, but there was no Jordan. He flew down the next day on a private jet and arrived at the arena with an armada of limousines carrying his security force of 20 to help hold back the crowds.

That Sunday, Michael wore jersey number 45, his minor league and junior high number, instead of the number 23 that he had made so famous. Number 23 was the last number his father James saw him compete in, Jordan later explained, and he wanted to keep it that way.

Champion, the sportswear manufacturer that holds the NBA license for jerseys, immediately added an extra shift and began producing more than 200,000 No. 45's for sale around the world.

Jordan played against Indiana like someone who had taken two years off. He made just 7 of 28 shots, but his defensive intensity helped the Bulls take the division-leading Pacers to overtime before losing. Afterward, Jordan broke his silence to address the hoopla of the preceding 10 days. "I'm human," he said. "I wasn't expecting this. It's a little embarrassing."

He said he had taken his time evaluating his love of the game and had come to the conclusion that it was real. That, he said, was the reason he returned, not financial considerations. He pointed out that the league had a moratorium on renegotiating contracts while it worked out a new labor agreement with the NBA Players Association, so he was required to play for the $3.9 million salary he left behind in 1993. (Although not required to, the Bulls had paid his full salary for 1993-94, and they would cover the full amount for 1994-95, although Jordan only played a portion of the season.) He also added that he had received no assurances about Pippen or Armstrong, although he asked.

His return, he said, was based solely on his love for basketball.

"I wanted to instill some positives back into this game," he said of his return, indicating his displeasure at some of the NBA's highly paid young players. "There's been a lot of negatives lately, young guys not taking care of their part of the responsibility, as far as the love of the game. I think you should love this game, not take advantage of it. . . be positive people and act like gentlemen, act like professionals."

Three nights later, he scored 27 points by shooting nine of 17 from the floor in a win over the Celtics at Boston Garden. Next would come a last-second shot for a win against Atlanta, and a 55-point performance against the awestruck Knicks in Madison Square Garden. Between these displays of greatness, he struggled through bouts of very ordinary play. Regardless, in a few short games he had served notice that he was indeed back.

It seemed the only question to be answered was whether he could still soar high enough to carry the Bulls to another title. Or was he now a mere mortal?

AFFAIRS OF THE HEART

SALT LAKE CITY, UTAH, APRIL 1995

When Jerry Sloan was an NBA player, he was known for his intensity, for being the kind of guy who would lay his heart on the line each and every game night. Now, he coaches the Utah Jazz, and star forward Karl Malone says that Sloan is still so intense most nights you can't touch him in the huddle.

"He's just a very competitive guy," Utah Jazz broadcaster Hot Rod Hundley says of Sloan. "That's the way he played. That's the way he coaches. Jerry believes that you play as hard as you can," Hundley says. "If the players respond and play hard, that's all he cares about. If you've done everything you can, and you play it straight and compete, there's nothing more you can ask for. That's what he demands. That's why he's had great teams every year. He'll win at least 55 games every year. The players love him. He gets the ultimate out of 99 percent of these guys. He gets them to play hard." John Stockton, Utah's point guard, says that he owes a special debt to Sloan, his coach since 1988, the longest coaching tenure in the NBA today. It's not unusual for a coach and a point guard to burn out their relationship over the course of a single season. But not Sloan and Stockton. "He is a great guy, a great competitor," Stockton says. "He's been in the player's shoes. I've thoroughly enjoyed playing with him, playing for him. I hope that that situation never changes over my career. He has constant influence on me with the little things that he says, things that you need to relax about, things that you need to fire up for, things that he remembered as a player that maybe hit home with me."

Unfortunately, Sloan's experience as a player all too closely mirrors what his Jazz players have faced in recent seasons. Like the Chicago teams Sloan used to play for, his Utah squads have lacked a dominating center, which means they have played well each year during the regular season only to struggle in the playoffs.

Since 1989, Sloan's teams, featuring Stockton and Malone, have averaged 54 wins a season, and twice (in 1991 and 1994) his Jazz have made it to the Western Conference Finals. But three other times they have lost in the first round of the playoffs. Such frustrations would probably get the best of lesser men. But Sloan doesn't even acknowledge the frustration, probably because acknowledging the frustration would mean acknowledging defeat. And he's just not going to do that.

MR. CHICAGO BULL

Hard as it may be to believe, long before Michael Jordan arrived on the scene, Jerry Sloan was known as Mr. Chicago Bull. At 6-6, he was a big guard, known for his defense and rebounding. Born into a family of 10 children (his father died when Sloan was four) and raised on a farm in the hardscrabble oil fields of southern Illinois, he played briefly at the University of Illinois and at Southern Illinois before transferring to Evansville in the early 1960s, where he led the team to two NCAA Division II national championships. Selected by the old Baltimore Bullets in the second round of the 1965 NBA draft, he played one season with Baltimore before being nabbed by Chicago in the 1966 expansion draft. Just a few games into that season, the Bullets approached Chicago about trading Sloan back to Baltimore. "No, a thousand times no," Bulls owner Dick Klein told them. "We're going to keep Jerry. I knock on wood every time I see him."

Over an 11-year NBA career, Sloan averaged 14 points and 7.4 rebounds, but his real contribution, his intense defense, escaped statistical analysis.

"Jerry was always an excitable person," said Johnny "Red" Kerr, who played with Sloan in Baltimore and coached him in Chicago. "I roomed with him in Baltimore on occasion. We'd play a game, and I'd go out for a couple of drinks and a sandwich. I'd come back at maybe one, two o'clock in the morning. I'd have the light off and be taking off my jacket. I'd see this glow of a cigarette in the dark. Jerry would be sitting up on the other bed, and he'd say, 'Red, remember that play in the third quarter?' I'd be getting ready for bed. I'd already had a couple of beers, and I'd forgotten about what happened in the third quarter because there was another game tomorrow. But he was so intense he wanted to know why we did certain things in certain situations. That really impressed me, and when I learned I was coming to Chicago as the coach I knew he was gonna be one of the players I'd take in the expansion draft. He didn't get a lot of playing time with the Bullets, but I saw him every day in practice. Nobody wanted any part of him. I knew the intensity he had.

"When I was coming to Chicago," Sloan recalled, "Johnny Kerr told me, 'You're kind of like a spring that's wound too tight. You might just fly all over the place. You don't want to get that wound up.' I worked hard on trying not to get that way. But I had those tendencies. That's the only way I could compete. I wasn't good enough, in my mind, unless I maintained a high level of intensity.

"When I left Baltimore, I didn't know if I'd be able to play in this league or not. I was drafted fairly high, but I didn't play much in Baltimore and started to have doubts. Two weeks before I went to Chicago, my brother shot himself. I had gotten myself mentally ready to play. But I was concerned because I hadn't worked out for a week because of my brother's funeral. Fortunately, I was in great shape. I could play hard every minute in training camp, and I got a little confidence. From that point, Johnny Kerr gave me more confidence by allowing me to play."

The arrival of Dick Motta as Bulls coach in Sloan's third season in Chicago created a perfect match of competitive attitudes.

"When we had our first training camp, it took about 10 minutes to recognize that he was very special," Motta remembered. "There weren't many players that had his intensity. I began to depend on him more out of necessity than anything. It was a natural evolution. He approached his play like he was desperate. One time at a clinic I heard him say, 'When I put the shoes on I get nervous because it might be the last time I'll ever get to put 'em on. So I want to play the best game I've ever played or have the best practice I've had.' He typified that his whole career."

If there was any part of his play that exemplified this intensity, it was his insistence on taking charges. Motta put together perhaps the most intimidating backcourt in the league in the 1970s when he teamed Sloan with Norm Van Lier, another hard-nosed defensive guard. Before long, opponents were complaining that Sloan and Van Lier were getting favorite treatment from the refs, that they would actually pull people on top of them to get charging fouls.

"There were no two tougher guards in basketball than Sloan and Van Lier," said Jeff Mullins, who played for the Golden State Warriors. "They were extremely competitive, very physical guys, the kind who would knock you down, then pick you up. They were always trying to draw the charge.

I'll never forget. We had a rookie form North Carolina named Bobby Lewis. When we played the Bulls, I told him, 'Bobby, you gotta watch Sloan and Van Lier because when you give the ball up and cut through, they'll sorta get you by the jersey and pull you down with them.' Lewis sort of half-listened to me and went in the game. Sure enough, he comes down the first time, and Jerry pulled him right over. Charge. The next time Lewis came down the other side and cut through. Norm Van Lier stepped in front. Another charge. A few minutes later Sloan got him again. Lewis got three straight charges without the ball and went bananas and had to sit down."

"Norm and I were very similar," Sloan admitted. "We were both crazy when it came to playing. Your hands have gotta be faster than the eye. We always had to have some means of taking people's minds off the game when they were on offense. Otherwise, they'd have just run by us like a layup drill if we'd let them play."

"A lot of those charges were legit," Van Lier says now. "A lot of people didn't have the guts to do it. A lot of those charges were hard, sure-enough, red-dog hits. But I took charges. I didn't pull you down. I wasn't strong enough to do that."

"I had the misfortune of having to play against Norm and Jerry Sloan," says Hall of Famer Nate "Tiny" Archibald, a guard for the old Cincinnati Royals. "Chicago was the toughest team to prepare for. We had some duels. They always outdid us. I remember we called our division the Black-and-Blue Division, mainly because we played against Chicago. I really didn't want them to physically beat me up, so I had to outrun those guys. A lot of people said they flopped on defense, but they were just guys that were glued to people...I'd get past Norm. The next thing I knew, Jerry Sloan was in my face. They had that great mentality about guarding people. They had pride."

"Jerry was gonna give you a day's work every day he came into the gym," said Bulls teammate Bob Love. "As hard as he was, when he was on the floor, if you blew on him he would fall back and grab you on the way down to take the charge. The game I remember about Sloan, we were playing New York in Chicago Stadium. The Knicks had Willis Reed and Earl Monroe and Walt Frazier and those guys. Willis Reed got a rebound and threw it out and was gonna beat Boerwinkle down the floor. He was hauling it down the floor. He had his head down, and when he looked up, Jerry Sloan was right there, man. He ran over Sloan. Charge! Willis fell on the floor and hurt his knee. He already had a bad knee. He looked at Jerry and said, 'Motherf----r, don't get in front of me again. You made me hurt my knee.' You know how guys talk. Sloan said, 'I ain't afraid of you.'

"Later in the game, Willis Reed got another rebound. He hauled off down the sideline again. This time he saw Jerry. Willis didn't go right, and he didn't go left. He ran over Jerry. When he hit Jerry, he walked all up to his head and scraped him and left Converse marks, from his forehead all the way down to his ear, man. All you saw was a red mark. And there was Willis saying, 'I told you not to get in front of me!' Sloan said, 'Motherf----r, I still ain't scared of you.'

"And the rest of the game, every time Willis got a rebound, he looked. He looked for Jerry. Jerry would have guys zigzagging down the floor, because you couldn't touch him. He was the greatest charge taker that I have ever seen in my life. You couldn't touch him, because he'd just fall back. Unbelievable.

"Jerry would make guys so mad," Love said. "Right now he would be considered the all-time greatest defensive player the game has ever known if he was playing on TV. He would have every kid in America copying that style. I loved the way the guy played. I was so happy I played with him and Norm Van Lier, because they made other guys so angry the way they played. The two best defensive guards in the history of the game, and they played on the same team. The best. Norm and Jerry were out there like two rats, and if the ball fell on the floor, it was like a piece of cheese. Those guys would undercut you, overcut you, clip you, do anything they could to get that ball. And they would get it, boy. And Dick Motta just loved it. He loved those guys. They really kept us pumped up."

"Jerry and I used to have our battles when we played against each other," said NBC broadcaster Matt Guokas, who played with and against Sloan. "Jerry is a unique defender in that he did not get up and put a lot of pressure on you, but he played angles, played position very well. He would make you do a lot of things you didn't want to do, but he didn't do it with pressure. Jerry was an excellent team defensive player and rebounder. When I played against him, we would get tangled up underneath the basket. There would be some elbow throwing, and we got in each other's face a couple of times. I was very happy to be on the same team with him. He was very demanding that you did certain things defensively, that you played hard, and that you got on the floor for loose balls and stepped up and took charges.

"That, of course, was the other thing about playing against Jerry," Guokas said. "He used to flop. He'd pull you on top of him and get you in foul trouble with a lot of charges. You wouldn't get away with that in today's game. There's still a lot of flopping that goes on but you couldn't put your arms around a guy and pull him down. Let me put it this way: They got away with it when I was on the other team, but when I was on the Bulls it seems they got called for it. Jerry was the consummate team player. Everyone that played with Jerry respected him. He was always in pain with a very bad groin injury. He would not get it stretched out before practice, yet he would go out and practice very hard for about an hour, which was all you could get out of anybody."

"Jerry and Norm Van Lier would just jump in front of you," said former Bulls guard Bob Weiss. "Jerry would take the hit. His weight would be on his heels, so it didn't take a whole lot to knock him over. But a charge is a charge. I think the term 'flopping' was basically an excuse for these guys they were drawing the fouls from. Jerry and Van Lier were very, very good at it. Jerry mostly. He was always getting in somebody's way and taking the punishment."

Like the Jazz teams Sloan later coached, the Bulls of the 1970s — featuring Love and Chet Walker at forward, Tom Boerwinkle and Clifford Ray at center and Sloan and Van Lier in the backcourt — would regularly win 50 games a season.

"Nobody could quite figure out why we were so successful," recalled former Bulls general manager Pat Williams, now an executive with the Orlando Magic. "Dick Motta used to say, 'When people look at this team, they forget the one key ingredient — the size of Jerry Sloan's heart.' Jerry Sloan was just fearless. His body would take such a pounding. In all my 28 years in the league, the player I most admire is Sloan. I've never been around a greater competitor, a more focused guy, a guy who cared as much...

"He's the only guy I've ever seen who played with his fists," Williams said. "He had huge hands. When he'd go for the ball on a steal, he'd punch it. He'd punch the ball right out of your hands. There's never been another Sloan. Never will be."

"My second year in Chicago we had to make up a game," Dick Motta recalled. "We had a game snowed out, and the league put it right at the end of the season. We had to play five games in five nights, and we needed to win four of them to make the playoffs. We beat Boston and Detroit in Chicago, then beat Milwaukee in a game played at Madison, Wisconsin. But with about a minute to go in the game, Lew Alcindor came out from behind a screen and knocked Jerry down. Jerry broke two ribs and separated his sternum. We had to bus down from Madison to O'Hare Airport after that Sunday afternoon game to catch a flight to Omaha to play Cincinnati for a game Monday night. So we had a doctor meet us at the airport. He basically told us that Sloan shouldn't go, that he should stay home. But Jerry insisted on going just to be with the team. We just needed one more win. The next day I went to the arena, and Sloan was there. He said, 'I couldn't sleep. I've been walking around. I've found this little corset thing. Let me warm up.'

"I said, 'No, I'm not gonna let you,'" Motta recalled. "He said, 'Coach, you gotta let me warm up.' So he warmed up, and I went back to the locker room. Later, I came out a little early, and he came up to me and said, 'You know I've never asked you to do one thing. I've never told you to do one thing. I'm gonna ask for one favor now.'

"I said, 'What's that, Jerry?'

"He said, 'If I were you, I'd start me.'

"I started him," Motta said, "and he couldn't raise his arm. Chet Walker and I had to stretch the uniform to get him in it. His ribs were broken, but he just wouldn't quit. We were down three early in the second half, and Cincinnati called a quick time-out. In the huddle, Jerry said, 'C'mon guys, let's go. We've come from 33 down before.'

"I looked up at the clock and said, 'Jerry, what's wrong?'

"He said, 'Oh, I thought we were down 33.'

"The pain was so excruciating he was incoherent," Motta said. "He was going on an empty tank. We won the game in overtime, and made the playoffs. I was able to rest Jerry the last game, and he played in the playoffs. So it was easy to build a team around that type of performance. He had a bad game once. I think his sister-in-law had died, and he went down to Evansville to the funeral and wasn't going to make it back. But he rented a small plane and got there about three minutes before tipoff. Chet Walker looked at him and said, 'I thought you weren't gonna play tonight.'

"He said, 'I couldn't miss it.'

"Chet said, 'You're a hell of a guy, Jerry.'

"And that's how everyone perceived Jerry," Motta said. "No coach and player had a relationship like Jerry and I had. It was very special. He was my sounding board, my assistant coach the first four years when I didn't have an assistant coach. So I would bounce trades off of him. I bounced all of our deals off of Jerry. I felt it was more his team than it was mine. He was an incredible guy. He still is."

"Sloan and Dick were like brothers," former Bull Gar Heard said. "It was like blood. They had such a great love for each other. Even now. I don't think anything could come between them. Sloan was the one guy who would play every night. On some nights I didn't see how he walked out on the floor. He was so banged up with his knees and stuff. But every night he came on the floor you knew he was gonna get it on."

"They retired Sloan's number 4 in Chicago," Motta said. "I don't know if he'll ever be in the Hall of Fame, but he should be."

The closest the Bulls came to playing for the championship was the 1975 Western Conference Finals, where they took a 3-2 lead over the Golden State Warriors. Ironically, the Bulls had traded Clifford Ray to the Warriors for center Nate Thurmond, the dominating center they thought they needed. But Ray's rebounding and defense played a key role in defeating his former teammates.

Sloan's playing career ended a few months later with a knee injury early in the 1975-76 season. He was a two-time All Star and four times was named to the league's All-Defensive first team and twice to the All-Defensive second team. After his playing days, he accepted the job as head coach at Evansville, his alma mater, only to change his mind and resign five days later. That fall of 1977, just months after his resignation, the Evansville team and coaching staff were killed in a plane crash. Just a week earlier he had visited with the Evansville players when they played in Chicago against DePaul, and the incident left him badly shaken for many months.

Instead of coaching in college, Sloan became an assistant with the Bulls and was named the team's head coach in 1979. The owners had picked him thinking he was the man to lead the team out of its years of frustration. But he had trouble adjusting his intensity.

"There was a real sense of excitement with his hiring," recalled Tim Hallam, the Bulls longtime PR man. "The owners thought Jerry Sloan would be the one guy who could rectify this stuff. But they just kept bringing in young guys and draft picks, and none of them worked out."

"I wasn't ready to be a coach, obviously," Sloan says. "But since I'd played here I figured if I had the right people around me to help me out, I had a better feeling for all the things that were going on here and some of the problems you were gonna have to deal with."

"Jerry was a wild man," recalled former Bulls trainer Mark Pfeil. "His idea was, things don't have to be complicated if you lay your heart on the line every night. And that's the way he coached."

"Some guys did not like Jerry," said former Bull Ronnie Lester, now a scout for the Lakers. "Not that he was a tough guy to play for. But he demanded things of his players. He would get in players' faces and challenge them personally, and a lot of players did not like that and did not take well to it."

"You have to have intensity to a certain point," Sloan says of coaching, "but it can be very damaging to you. The intensity I had as a player, it was hard to put aside as a coach. Early in my career, any question from other people seemed to be more of a challenge than anything else. I probably took it that way. That was very difficult for me. I wanted everything to be perfect. I didn't realize that it wasn't going to be."

"Sloan's first Chicago team finished 30-52, and for his second year, the team brought in free agent forward Larry Kenon, who had averaged about 20 points and 10 rebound for San Antonio. Almost immediately, the two began feuding.

"Jerry was such a straightforward, stand-up guy," Hallam said. "This in the days before coaches began using the phoniness and coddling and bull that it took to keep players happy. Jerry wasn't coddled as a person, didn't expect it, and wasn't going to give it. I think he got along with his kind of players. He didn't get along with Larry Kenon. When I met Larry Kenon, I said, 'Hello, Larry.' He said, 'Larry is my slave name. People call me K. or Dr. K.'

Sloan benched Kenon, then proceeded to coach the Bulls into the 1981 playoffs, where they upset the New York Knicks in the first round and lost to the Boston Celtics in the conference semifinals. But the next season, when the team started 19-32, general manager Rod Thorn fired Mr. Chicago Bull.

"Firing Jerry was one of the toughest things I've ever done because I have a lot of respect for him," Thorn says now. "He works very hard, is a stand-up guy. He doesn't make excuses. He does everything he can do and is always there. He never bails out."

Hallam remembers that the day Sloan was fired he agreed to meet with reporters. He answered every single question that day and made no excuses for his lack of success.

"They'd always paid me on the first and the fifteenth," Sloan said of the Bulls. "That's one of the things I'd always appreciated. That's life. Because we're in sports we think we deserve a little bit more than that, but we really don't."

The toughest part of the firing was explaining to his kids that everything was going to be all right, that the world wasn't going to end just because he wasn't with the Bulls.

Sure enough, he landed a job coaching in the Continental Basketball Association. Then Frank Layden brought him to Utah as an assistant coach, where he has remained ever since.

Now, as yet another spring comes to the Rockies, Sloan prepares to face the playoffs once again. The Jazz have played well over the spring, winning 60 games for the first time in their history. But deep in Sloan's gut, there's probably a terrible knot of anxiety. He probably sits alone at night after a loss, smoking in the dark, thinking about errant plays. But he'll never admit to any such anxiety.

To Jerry Sloan, the answer to the question is as simple as it was 50 years ago, when he was a kid on that southern Illinois farm, after his father had died, leaving a family of 10 to fend for themselves.

You lay your heart on the line.

Night after night. Game after game. Then you get up the next day and start it all over again.

END GAME

THE 1995 NBA PLAYOFFS

As the 1995 NBA Playoffs set to open, the coaching staff of the Chicago Bulls gathered in their war room at their practice facility, the Berto Center, in northwest suburban Chicago, to study their first-round opponent — the Charlotte Hornets.

Assistant coach Jim Cleamons had broken down videotape of the Hornets into a scouting report. Immediately the Bulls staff — head coach Phil Jackson and assistants Tex Winter, Cleamons and Jimmy Rodgers — noted the influence of former Bulls assistant coach Johnny Bach on Charlotte's defense.

But it was the Charlotte offense — particularly the Hornets' main weapons, Larry Johnson and Alonzo Mourning — that most interested the Bulls coaches. One of their first observations was that Mourning, the 6-10 center, was somewhat clumsy and traveled nearly every time he got the ball in the post.

"He walks on everything," complained the 73-year-old Winter, the mastermind of Chicago's famed triple-post offense. "He's got big ol' feet. He can't help but walk."

Cleamons had included a selection of tape showing Mourning caught in a triple team yet forcing up a terrible shot instead of passing. "He wants to be the hero," Cleamons noted.

Mourning's shortcomings aside, the Bulls knew they would have to double-team him, and the logical man to leave open would be second-year swing player Darrin Hancock, who had a suspect outside shot.

"Mourning will still have all of our post guys in foul trouble," cautioned Winter, an inveterate worrier.

"That's all right. We have 18 fouls to give," Jackson said, referring to Chicago centers Luc Longley, Will Perdue and Bill Wennington, who would come to be known as a "three-headed monster" in reference to the Bulls' hopes that the three of them could counter other team's top centers.

"But Mourning's a good foul shooter," Winter said, not satisfied.

Cleamons, one of Jackson's old teammates with the New York Knicks, stepped to the chalk board and pointed out that the Hornets' offense often seemed muddled. "We'll be okay if we keep Johnson and Mourning out of the middle," he said. "But if we let them in the middle we'll have to use our fouls."

He also pointed out that the Hornets' attack was severely limited by the absence of point guard Muggsy Bogues, who had been battling injuries for several weeks. "Without Muggsy, they have no running game," Cleamons said. "They have to resort to post-ups and isolations and individual talent."

Winter wasn't so confident. "We got to figure how to keep the ball out of that guy's hands," he said of Mourning.

Such debate is a welcomed and critical element for the Bulls' coaching staff, which has been built around Winter's voluminous knowledge. Winter has been the head coach at five colleges — Marquette, Kansas State, Washington, Northwestern and Long Beach State — and has served as head coach of the San Diego/Houston Rockets. His specialty over the years had been the development of the triple-post offense, which figured greatly in the Bulls' three championship seasons. One of Jerry Krause's first acts upon being named Bulls general manager in 1985 was to phone Winters, his old mentor, and offer him a job as assistant coach.

It was a source of irritation to Krause that the first two head coaches he hired — Stan Albeck and Doug Collins — decided not to follow Winter's offensive advice. If they had, they just might have kept their jobs. It wasn't until Krause hired Jackson in 1989 that he found a coach willing to listen to Winter. As a result, Winter's first four years with the club featured some trying times. During the 1988-89 season, the discord on the coaching staff got so bad that Collins blocked Winter from coming to practice.

"Tex was basically out of the picture at that time," Jackson recalled. "He did some scouting for Jerry Krause and took some road trips. He didn't go on all of our game trips. When he was with us, he sat in a corner and kept notes on practice and didn't participate in the coaching. He was out of it."

"Tex is like a grandpa to all of us," says former Bulls trainer Mark Pfeil. "But the players would mock him. Michael used to tease him and stuff. Over everything. One time in practice, Michael sneaked up behind him and pulled Tex's shorts all the way down to his knees, and there was Tex's bare butt sticking out."

The Bulls players may not have always taken Winter with complete seriousness during the early years, but once Jackson arrived and let it be known that the team was using Winter's offensive system, that all changed.

"Michael's sort of his own man," Winter says of Jordan. "I think he's talked to Phil occasionally about what we do offensively and how he fits into the scheme of things. I let Phil handle that. My basic job is of teacher. When we step out on that floor at a practice session, I'm going to coach whoever shows up. And I'm going to coach them the way I coach, whether it's Michael Jordan, Scottie Pippen, or Pete Myers or whoever it is. It doesn't make any difference. They know that. If I see Michael making a mistake, I'll correct him as fast as I will anyone else. On the other hand, he's such a great athlete you have to handle him a little differently than you do the other players. I don't think you can come down on him hard in a very critical way, whereas some younger guy or some other guy you feel you might me able to motivate by coming down on them pretty tough."

Even so, Winter's elevated status with Jackson's arrival didn't mean that the team stopped seeing him as grandfatherly. "Tex is a few years younger than my parents and a product of that Depression era," says current Bulls trainer Chip Schaefer. "To say that he is frugal would be an understatement. Johnny Bach used to call him penurious. I think that's a very apt description of him. But I think Tex in a lot of ways is the way we all should be. He doesn't like to see things get wasted. He takes that attitude at the dinner table, too. If there's a little bit of meat on your bone, he may just pick up your steak bone and finish it off for you."

"The teaching is the reward for me," Winter says. "You get a big thrill watching a guy like (former Bulls journeyman) Pete Myers grow in the scheme of things. You can take a role player and see how they fit in our system of play. You can see their improvement, especially with a guy like Will Perdue, who's really had a struggle with some of the things we do."

"Basketball is his absolute passion in life," Schaefer says. "He's 73 years old, and that's what keeps him going. There's times when he'll look tired, and I'll wonder if he has the energy for it. Then all of a sudden practice will start and he's out here barking at these guys like he's coaching the K-State freshman team and it's 1948. Tex has 3 or 4 real passions in life. One of them's basketball. Certainly one of them's food. He really enjoys his finances. He pores over the business section of the paper as intensely as he does the sports section. He's a real joy. I hope he keeps on going."

After the coaches' April afternoon skull session, Winter headed down to the deserted Berto Center press room to scavenge for free newspapers and check the change holders in the vending machines. Sifting through a stack of discarded newspapers, he scanned the days headlines, all of which dealt with the bombing of the federal building in Oklahoma City.

I asked him what should be done with the bombers when they are caught.

"Hang 'em up by the balls," he said flatly.

MAVERICK

It is the war room in the Bulls' Berto Center that perhaps most reflects the personality and philosophy of Phil Jackson. For starters, American Indian art is the room's dominant motif, an outgrowth of Jackson's spiritual mysticism that incorporates strains of Zen Buddhist and Native American teachings.

The son of a Pentecostal preacher, Phil Jackson was raised in Montana. By the end of high school, he longed for relief from his strict upbringing. He found escape in an athletic scholarship at the University of North Dakota, where he played basketball for an engaging young coach named Bill Fitch. The 6-foot-8 Jackson developed into a two-time NCAA Division II All-American, a legitimate pro prospect, the only problem being that few pro scouts found their way out to North Dakota. One who did was a chubby young Baltimore Bullets representative named Jerry Krause, who was entertained by Fitch's trick of having Jackson sit in the back seat of a Chevrolet and use his long arms to grab the steering wheel or unlock the front doors on either side. "I had quite a wingspan," Jackson recalled with a chuckle.

After his 13-year playing career with the Knicks, Jackson worked as an assistant coach and broadcaster for the New Jersey Nets before moving on to become head coach of the Albany Patroons in the Continental Basketball Association for five seasons. In 1984, Jackson's Patroons won the CBA title, and the next season he was named CBA coach of the year. He was doing a brief stint coaching in Puerto Rico when Jerry Krause contacted him about an assistant coaching job with the Bulls in 1985. Most NBA general managers would never have considered him head coaching material.

"I thought I was ready to be an NBA coach at age 35," Jackson recalled. "I had served two years as an NBA assistant in New Jersey. But I really didn't have a clue then, and I know that now. So I went to the CBA and had some success, but still nothing came in my direction. I had no mentor in the NBA. My coach when I played with the Knicks, Red Holtzman, had retired and was out of the game. Although Dave DeBusschere, my former Knicks teammate, was a general manager, he had no control over my destiny as a coach. Jerry Krause was like the only person that really stayed in touch with me from the NBA world. And he had just gotten back in it. But that was my connection. Jerry had seen me play in college, and we had a relationship that spanned 20 years."

Jackson was known as something of a strange duck during his playing days with the New York Knicks. In *Maverick*, his 1975 autobiography written with Charlie Rosen for Playboy Press, Jackson recalled his exploration of sixties counterculture, including candid accounts of drug use. The book was an excellent basketball tome as well as a personal story of spiritual growth. It was not, however, the type of book commonly associated with a head coach or authority figure.

"The only thing in that book that's an embarrassment for me today," Jackson said, "is that people have picked out one or two phrases and said, 'This is who Phil Jackson is.' Sportswriters in the past have seized on one experience with psychedelic drugs or some comments I've made about the type of lifestyle I had as a kid growing up in the '60s and '70s. I've tried to make sure people don't just grab a sentence or phrase to build a context for someone's personality."

"I've never read the book," Krause says. "I didn't need to. I knew about Phil's character. Besides, I'd hired other colorful personalities before."

Yet perhaps no one quite so colorful as Jackson. Shortly after coming to the Bulls in 1985, Krause called Jackson to interview with new Bulls head coach Stan Albeck for the job of assistant coach.

"I was coaching in Puerto Rico," Jackson recalled, "and I flew up directly from San Juan. It was a quick trip. I had to drive into San Juan and catch a morning flight. When you live in the subtropics, you get a lifestyle. I was wearing flip-flops most of the time. I wore chino slacks, because of their social standards down there, and a polo shirt. I had an Ecuadorian straw hat. Those hats are really expensive. They're not like a Panama, which costs 25 bucks. It's a $100 hat. You could crush proof it. As a little flair item, I had a parrot feather that I'd picked up at a restaurant. I had messed around with a macaw in the restaurant and pulled a tail feather out and stuck it in my hat.

"There was a certain image I presented. I had a beard, had had it for a number of years. I was a little bit of an individualist, as I still am. I have a certain carriage about myself that's going to be unique. I just came in for the interview. I don't know how it affected Stan Albeck. Stan was a good coach. He'd been around and had some success.

"Stan and I had a very short interview. It wasn't very personal, and I knew right away that Stan wasn't looking to hire me, although Jerry Krause had locked us in a room and said, 'I want you guys to sit down and talk X's and O's.' Stan found a different topic to talk about."

"Stan came back to me after the interview," Krause recalled, "and said, 'I don't want that guy under any circumstances.' When we brought Phil in again to interview for the assistant's job two years later, I told him what to wear. And to shave."

Krause fired Stan Albeck after a season, then hired Doug Collins and brought Jackson in as an assistant. In 1989, when he fired Collins, Krause promoted Jackson. "One of Jerry Krause's greatest decisions that he gets no credit for was finding Phil Jackson in the CBA," observed Bulls chairman Jerry Reinsdorf.

"I had kept up with Phil as a player through the years," Krause recalled. "We'd talk from time to time, and I followed his coaching career in the CBA. When I got the job (as general manager) in Chicago in 1985, I talked to him again. I told him I needed scouting reports on the CBA. Within a week, I had typewritten reports on the whole league, detail on every player. What I saw in Phil was an innate brightness. I thought that eventually he'd become the governor of North Dakota. I saw a lot of Tony LaRussa in him. A feel for people. A brightness. Question asking. A probing mind. A coach."

"My first two years as an assistant coach with the Bulls, it was very much like going to graduate school," Jackson says. "My first year here I was hired after my children were already in school and my wife had a job. So my family stayed in Woodstock (New York, his home at the time). I had a lot of free hours to spend learning basketball from Johnny Bach (the Bull's other veteran assistant at the time) and Tex Winter. There was Tex's western input and Johnny's eastern input. So I got about 30 years of basketball history real quick."

Jackson had been a member of the Knicks when they won the NBA title in 1973. Yet Jackson actually cites the Knicks' 1970 season, when he was on the injured list after undergoing major back surgery, as the breakthrough season in his pro basketball career. That year he sat in the stands at Madison Square Garden watching Knicks' coach Red Holtzman's every move. It was then, Jackson wrote in *Maverick*, that he came to understand the game. That season also laid the foundation for the philosophy he sought to instill when he became head coach of the Bulls.

"The Knicks in the late '60s and early '70s were one of the dominant teams in the NBA," Jackson says, "yet they were a collection of very good individual players without a dominant star that could change the context of the game.

"The whole idea of the Knicks playing together was how well the ball moved, how well they played together defensively, the fact that any of the five players could take a key shot down the stretch. It was a difficult team in that regard to defend against. They were unselfish, and Red Holtzman, the mentor, was really the guy who taught us that. Surprisingly enough, he taught us teamwork through defense."

Before purchasing the Bulls, Reinsdorf, a Brooklyn native, had been an intense Knicks' fan. Upon acquiring the team, he wanted that kind of philosophy instilled in Chicago. Jackson proved to be just the coach to make it happen. "That was the concept when I came to the Bulls, that the ball had to move," Jackson says. "They all had to touch the ball regardless of who was gonna score. Everybody had to become interdependent upon each other and trusting on the offensive end. Defensively, we were gonna play full court pressure. We were gonna make defense where we started our teamwork."

"I think Phil came in with the basis of some very sound philosophy," Winter says. "I mean the philosophy of life. He recognizes that there are a whole lot of things more important than basketball. He doesn't take himself too seriously. We all take basketball pretty seriously at times. Even then, he's inclined to relax. I'm amazed at times in the course of the game how he sits back and lets things happen. He likes people to be able to solve their own problems, and so he gives his players the reins. On the other hand, when he sees they're out of control, then he starts to pull them in a little bit. I think this is his strength, the way he handles the players and his motivation, his personal relationship with the players. That's borne out by the fact that they'll accept his coaching, they'll accept the criticism, even though sometimes it's pretty severe with certain players. They accept that because it's who he is, because he's Phil."

"I've always been impressed by Phil," says former Bulls guard John Paxson, a broadcaster for the team. "He's an intellectual guy, and I think that's the first thing that stood out to me. You don't run into too many intellectual guys in the NBA. The thing that impressed me is that he hasn't allowed this game to consume him. It can be so consuming for a coach. But Phil has other interests. He has other interests. His family has always been important to him. And he has never let the game take a toll on him mentally. When you're around him, you can see that he has a good mind, and whatever he chooses to apply it to, he's been good at it. He's a take control type of person, and when he was an assistant coach, you got the impression with Phil that someday he was going to get a job and be in control."

"I don't have Red Holtzman's wry sense of humor," Jackson says of his coaching abilities. "But I am able to give the players a certain sense of respect, a certain integrity. I have the sense to talk to them personally, instead of running them down as a group, or taking them down another notch in front of the group. I have the sense to take the time. Those were the things that Red taught me that were important."

Jackson's skill at establishing these relationships is no small feat, Winter says. "These pro players have all been the top players in the country in college. They've been recruited and on scholarship their whole lives, from junior high to college. These guys have tremendous egos. They have a lot of pride themselves. You're not going to pull the wool over their eyes, and the thing the coach has to do is win their respect. Phil has certainly done that."

Not long after taking the job, Jackson began passing out books to his players. A prodigious reader himself, he hoped some of them might find an avenue to personal growth. Most of the players looked at Jackson as if he'd lost his mind. A few, however, such as power forward Horace Grant, responded to the gesture. "That's the thing that makes coaching really enjoyable and fun for me. You need diversification," Jackson says. "If you have that, you can keep it interesting for these guys. There's a danger because you get on the treadmill of pro basketball. You just keep running on the treadmill and you can't get off. It's something that can be generated from a season to one year to 10 years to 20 years. You look at some of these guys, they've been around the game for 30 years. And they just stay in that same pattern. But you should try to make the pattern just a little bit better. Sometimes I think you have to jump off the treadmill, step back a little ways from it, relook it and rethink it."

While Jackson's philosophical touches distinguished him, it was his practical decisions that ultimately weighed in making the Bulls successful. By the time Jackson took over as head coach in 1989, Michael Jordan was 26 years old and facing explosive fame and wealth. His annual off-court income was ballooning from $4 million to $30 million. Overnight he had become a cultural icon. Just as Jordan struggled personally to cope with this newfound status, Bulls management feared the team might well be consumed by it, too.

"I was nervous when I took over the Bulls," Jackson admits, "but it wasn't the kind of nervousness where you lose sleep at night. I wanted to do well. I was anxious about having a good relationship with Michael. I was anxious about selling him on the direction in which I was going. You knew what Michael was going to give you every single night as a player. He was gonna get those 30 points; he was gonna give you a chance to win. The challenge was, how to get the other guys feeling a part of it, like they had a role, a vital part. It was just his team, his way.

"He had such hero worship in the United States among basketball fans that living with him had become an impossibility," Jackson says. "Traveling in airports, he needed an entourage to get through. He had brought people along on the road with him. His father would come. His friends would come on the road. He had just a life that sometimes alienated him from his teammates. It became a challenge to make him part of the team again and still not lose his special status because he didn't have the necessary privacy.

"I had roomed on the same floor of hotels as he did. Michael always had a suite because of who he was, and the coaches got suites, too, because we needed the space for team meetings and staff meetings. Michael basically had to have someone stay in his room with him. I'd hear murmuring in the hallway, and there'd be six or eight of the hotel staff, cleaning ladies, busboys, getting autographs and standing in the hallway with flowers. It was incredible, and he was constantly bothered. So I knew that we had to make exceptions to the basic rules that we had: 'Okay, so your father and your brothers and your friends can't ride on the team bus. Let's keep that a team thing. Yeah, they can meet you on the road, but they can't fly on the team plane. There has to be some of the team stuff that is ours, that is the sacred part of what we try to do as a basketball club.'

"I got a curtain for our practice facility, so that practice became our time together. It was just the 12 of us and the coaches, not the reporters and the television cameras. It wasn't going to be a show for the public anymore. It became who are we as a group, as people. Michael had to break down some of his exterior. You know that when you become that famous person you have to develop a shell around you to hide behind.

"Michael had to become one of the guys in that regard," Jackson says. "He had to involve his teammates, and he was able to do that. He was able to bring it out and let his hair down at the same time. Over his years in pro basketball, Michael had learned to mark out his own territory. He had his own stall at every arena where he might find the most privacy, or he might find a territory in the trainer's room. He had two stalls in the old Chicago Stadium. That was his spot because there were 25 reporters around him every night.

"We continued the protocol of all that, but we also made efforts to create space for him within the team. If we hadn't done that, the way he was going to treat us was that the rest of the world was going to overrun us, if we hadn't done things the right way. So we said, 'Let's not all suffer because of his fame. Let's give ourselves space and exclude the crowd.' I guess I created a safe zone, a safe space for Michael. That's what I tried to do."

"Phil's handled Michael so well," Paxson says. "If I could ever take a page out of the manual for handling a superstar, it would be the way Phil's handled Michael Jordan."

"Some nights he could take on a whole team," Jackson says of Jordan. "They'd say, 'That son of a gun, he beat us all to the basket.' As a coach, you can run that tape back all day. You say, 'Look at this guy go around that guy and that guy. He beat four guys going to the basket that time.' That's destructive. That's something that Michael's been known for, and I know it grates at the heart of the other team. It's an amazing feat this guy has been able to accomplish. But I think his power is very addictive. You know the fans were there looking for him. Everybody's waiting. They loved it. He had this tremendous vision of basketball. He was this tremendous entertainer."

"He lives in his own world a great deal," Winter says of Jordan. "I don't think he wants people to figure out what Michael Jordan's thinking. It's one of his strengths."

It was just one of many traits that left the Bulls' coaches in awe of Jordan, Jackson says. "After having a game that was mediocre or average, a game where maybe he did too much, a game that we lost, Michael had an ability to walk through the plane and say, 'Guys, we're gonna kick butt tomorrow. They're gonna have to beat us. They can't put it together.'

"That attitude, that tremendous competitiveness, sometimes makes it tough to be a teammate, because you see that tremendous competitiveness is gonna eat you up everywhere. It's gonna eat you up playing golf with him next week, playing cards with him next month. That attitude of arrogance is gonna be there. It's not always the best for personal connections and friendship. But it certainly makes for greatness."

But by 1989, Jordan's "greatness" had become an issue. Was he the kind of player who could lead a team to a championship? Or was he the kind of superstar whose gifts were good only for the show? The kind of player whose game tended to minimize his teammates? Those questions haunted and angered Jordan. He faced a strait gate. If he complained about the abilities of the players on the Bulls roster, he was seen as arrogant. If he tried to do too much himself, he was seen as a selfish ball hog. Never had his basketball skills been a question. But now his leadership skills, and his character, were. Unfortunately, there was only one way for Jordan to answer the questions and the criticism. He had to meld with Winter's and Jackson's philosophy of a team concept.

"I think there came a point where he understood his greatness was going to be defined by winning," Paxson says. "That's why I saw a change in his real commitment to winning championships and, to that end, dealing with teammates and getting guys he felt comfortable with, that were able to play with him. It was really that understanding that championships mean a lot when it comes down to who's the greatest. There are great NBA players who've never won championships, and it's always been a blot on their careers.

"Michael is easily the most demanding athlete I've been around, Paxson says. "I don't want any of that to sound like there's something wrong with that because there's not. There came a point in his career that winning championships was going to be one of the defining things in his career. He put more pressure on himself than he did on his teammates. As much pressure as he puts on guys around him he puts more on himself. That says a lot about him."

"I guess I expected more from a lot of them," Jordan said of his teammates. "But some of them didn't want to take more responsibility... We were inconsistent and I was frustrated."

"If you showed weakness around him, he'd run you off," Paxson says. "He was always challenging you in little ways. The thing you had to do with Michael Jordan is you had to gain his confidence as a player. You had to do something that gave him some trust in you as a player. He was hard on teammates as far as demanding you play hard, you execute. So there had to come some point where you did something on the floor to earn his trust. That was the hardest thing for new guys coming in, and some guys couldn't deal with it. Some guys could not play consistently enough or well enough, or they would not do the dirty work or little things. That's one of the reasons why Michael liked (former Bull) Charles Oakley because Charles played hard. He did little things on the floor that Michael appreciated, but a lot of guys didn't understand that.

"Michael demanded nothing less than playing hard. If you missed shots when you were open, he didn't want to see that either. If Michael came off the screen and roll a couple of times and threw a quick pass to

(Bulls center) Bill Cartwright and he couldn't handle it, Michael wasn't going to go there again. That was kind of what happened early. If you do something and one of your teammates doesn't respond to it you're going to think twice about going there. It's a natural thing. You always sensed with Michael that he was looking for perfection out of himself. There's a part of him that expected that of those around him, too."

It was Jackson's firm, yet understated style that helped bring the Bulls together, merging their great young superstar with a roster of role players, all loosely aligned in Winter's offensive system. Over the 1990-91 season, the Bulls became a picture of how basketball was meant to be played, a team of finesse and beauty. Once the parts fell into place, the Bulls ruled the league for three straight seasons. In the process, fans and opponents began to see the Maverick in an entirely different light. No longer just an oddball former player, he became what many consider the dean of NBA coaches.

"My father was a pastor," Jackson says. "Not only was he a pastor, he was superintendent for all the churches in the state of Montana. He had a certain carriage and a certain character about him that made him distinguishable. They say the apple doesn't fall far from the tree. I'll run into relatives, and they'll say, 'Gee, you look just like your Dad. The way you carry yourself, the way you speak to your team.' I'll get a kick out of that because there's a lot more anger and ire that goes into coaching than goes into the ministry. But there is something to it. All my life, I had to carry myself as a minister's son. I pulled a certain status. It makes a responsible position easy, things like wearing a suit and moving in crowds.

"Someone mentioned to me that when I address the media after a game it's almost like a sermon. I do think a lot about what I want to say about the games. We have a certain status as a basketball club that we have to carry, and I'm the representative of the Bulls. That's one of the other things that I think Michael Jordan does absolutely well. He has such a nice demeanor after a game. There's no blaming, no whining, no complaining.

"I get so many notes from fans who live in L.A. or Cleveland or New York. They say they've been fans of their local teams for years, but that the Bulls represent something they enjoy watching. I hope to think that some of that's my doing. I like to think I've helped build the character we have on this team."

Just when the Bulls seemed to be at the height of their power, trouble began to develop in their sleek machine. Jordan's father, James, was murdered in July 1993, leading to Michael's abrupt retirement that fall as training camp was set to open.

Led by Scottie Pippen, the team pulled together and won an amazing 55 games in 1993-94, but their championship run ended with a loss to the New York Knicks in the Eastern semifinals. In the aftermath, the team fired longtime assistant coach Johnny Bach, who had clashed with Krause.

"In essence, Johnny fired himself," Krause says of Bach's dismissal. "I told him many times that assistant coaches shouldn't be holding press conferences. Assistant coaches should have lower profiles. We cautioned him about that time and again, yet he kept doing it."

"Johnny was too friendly to the media, but he helped us," said Chicago radio reporter Cheryl Ray. "He gave us information, not to hurt the team. He would explain why something was being done and how it was working. In fact he would say to me, 'I can't talk to you. If management sees me, they'll get mad.' But the more they told him not to, the more he wanted to do it."

"It was Jerry Krause's relationship with Johnny Bach that created a very uncomfortable situation," Jackson says. "It made this have to happen eventually. It had gone all wrong. It was bad for the staff to have this kind of thing because we had to work together.

"Jerry basically blamed Johnny Bach for a lot of the things in the *Jordan Rules* (the controversial book by *Chicago Tribune* sportswriter Sam Smith). And there's no doubt that Johnny did provide that information. Jerry felt that Johnny talked too much. And Johnny, in retrospect, felt that animosity that Jerry gave back to him, the lack of respect, so Johnny refused to pay allegiance to Jerry just because he was the boss.

"It had gone on for too long a period of time," Jackson says. "I could have kept them apart, at bay from one another, I suppose for a while longer. But I didn't like the fact that it wasn't good teamwork. That was my staff and my area. I agreed to do it. I felt it was a good opportunity because Johnny had an opportunity to get another job in the league quickly. It worked out fine for Johnny, although I would just as soon have not put him through the disappointment, or have to go through the situation myself."

On the heels of Bach's dismissal, power forward Horace Grant left in an acrimonious exchange with Reinsdorf and Krause and moved to the Orlando Magic as a free agent.

Pippen, too, began feuding with management, leading to bitter public accusations that the team had lied to him, all of which left Jackson struggling to hold his club together. Just when it seemed he couldn't hold on much longer, Jordan announced his return to the Bulls in March, and suddenly the problems — Pippen's fight with management and the team's mediocre play — dissipated in the euphoria over Jordan's reappearance in Bulls uniform.

Jackson, however, was left struggling with mixed feelings about his relationship with Krause. Jackson had long considered the general manager his mentor. But he believed Krause was sometimes too demonstrative in dealing with the players.

At times, Krause would inquire about making a pep talk to the team, Jackson says. "He'll say, 'What if I go down (to the players) and say to these guys, 'We gotta get this one tomorrow.' How do you think that'll make them feel?' I'll say, 'Jerry, I don't know. I don't think that will really work.' A lot of times he'll check these things out with me before he does them."

Other times, however, Krause would charge right in, Jackson says. "The thing that happened with Pippen last year (the drawn out public infighting) was avoidable. The things that have happened in the past were avoidable. Somehow or other they got pushed to greater limits. But that's part of who Jerry is. He wants to directly confront when he feels that there has been a problem. He wants to challenge and overrun people and be brusque. He's very brusque and sets people on edge just by walking into the locker room sometimes. We've had to talk to him about his manner in the locker room. On the other hand, Jerry keeps his space very well. He doesn't overrun us, the coaches. He allows a coach to do what he wants to do as far as strategy and how he wants to handle the players. Jerry has a very good attitude about protocol.

"He's just a very unusual guy."

Krause had no comment about Jackson's complaint, other than to say that he is a bit mystified by Jackson's criticisms, saying he seldom seeks to even speak with the players, except for a brief talk at the beginning and end of each season. Yet these are Jackson's opinions, Krause says, and he is welcome to them.

Reinsdorf, for his part, sees a creative tension at work in the relationship between coach and general manager, and given its success in recent seasons, it would be hard to argue against it.

"Phil gets annoyed with Jerry from time to time," Reinsdorf says. "But Jerry is Phil's boss. Everybody gets annoyed with their bosses. Back when I had a boss I used to get annoyed with him. Whatever annoyances Phil feels, they're just petty annoyances."

Despite whatever internal tension the Bulls faced in April 1995, the circumstances of Jordan's return had engendered an overwhelming belief among Chicagoans that Michael was about to perform his grandest miracle of all: He would return after a two-year absence, play just 17 games of the regular season, then lead an undermanned Bulls team into the playoffs to capture a fourth title.

It had all the appeal of a storybook ending, which is what it proved to be. Instead of magic, Jordan's return created mostly unrealistic expectations. The Bulls finished in fifth place in the Eastern Conference and had no home-court advantage in the playoffs. Still, as Jim Cleamons had foreshadowed in his scouting session before the playoffs, the Bulls managed to oust the Charlotte Hornets in six games in the first round. But it became increasingly obvious that Jordan still lacked the stamina and timing to deliver a miracle.

In the second round, against the Orlando Magic with Shaquille O'Neal, Anfernee Hardaway and Horace Grant, the Bulls and Jordan found themselves out of sync, particularly in Game 1 in Orlando when Jordan committed two late turnovers that cost the Bulls the game. From there, Jordan missed shots, made miscues and watched Grant's play shift the balance in the series. At one point, Jordan donned his old jersey number 23 to get a second win, but the Magic took over from there to claim a 4-2 series victory.

"We agonized a little bit for him this year when he went through the postseason drama," Jackson said later. "But knowing Michael so well, I put my arm around him after that first game against Orlando when he lost the ball and said, 'As many times as we won behind you, I never expected to see this happen. Let's use it for our tool. Let's use it to build a positive. You're our guy, and don't ever forget that.' You never think you'll have to go to Michael and talk about something like that."

Bulls fans were understandably stunned by the turn of events. In the days following the loss, the sports radio talk show airwaves were filled with comments that the team needed to rework its approach, that the triple-post offense had outlived its usefulness.

Even Winter, the architect of the system, had his doubts. Jordan had never expressed an opinion to Winter about the triple-post. But now Winter wanted to know, so he implored Jackson to ask Jordan's opinion when the two met for the postseason interview that Jackson annually holds with each of his players.

"With his impulsiveness," Jackson recalled, "Tex said, 'Phil, I'd like you to ask him, does he think we need to change the offense? Can we play this triple-post offense? Is it something we should plan on using next year? I want you to ask him just for me.' So I did, and Michael said, 'The triple-post offense is the backbone of this team. It's our system, something that everybody can hang their hat on, so that they know where to go and how to operate.'"

UTAH

The Bulls weren't the only team to find a surprise ending to their season. After finishing with a franchise best 60 wins, two behind San Antonio in the Midwest, the Utah Jazz held high hopes for the playoffs. Strangely, Jerry Sloan's players noticed a newfound peace coming over their coach as the regular season wound to a close. "Jerry is doing the things now that I had always hoped he would do," Karl Malone said. "He'll still get in your face, but he'll also sit down on the bench and watch the game. It seems to me that he's enjoying the game more than he ever has.

"This is the best I've ever seen him coach, with a loss and a win. And now I can touch him on the shoulder during a game and he'll kind of smile at me sometimes, whereas in the past, he'd look at me like, 'What are you thinking about?' It's sort of neat to see him like that. He's still intense now, without a doubt. We got a motto: Once you suit up, you're ready to play. So he's intense, but now he also knows when to slack up a little bit, too."

As the playoffs began, this calm spread across the roster and combined with their winning streaks to give the Jazz perhaps the strongest confidence they'd ever had. "Do you think you can win it all?" a reporter asked John Stockton.

"Absolutely," he said. "We're just a good group of guys, hard-working guys who are committed to each other and to winning."

The same reporter asked Stockton when he was going to slow down.

"Hopefully never," the point guard replied. "Everything doesn't feel the way it felt 10 years ago. But I feel good. I feel I've been fortunate to stay somewhat injury free. I'll keep my fingers crossed and keep playing."

"People say if you can't win it this year that you and Karl Malone might be getting too old," the reporter asked. "What do you think?"

"They also said that four years ago," Stockton said. "I think our best chances have been in the last two or three years, including this one. This is our best chance yet. We're just gonna try to take advantage of that and not worry about the other part."

Ultimately, it wasn't age, but luck, that cost the Jazz in the playoffs. They drew the defending champion Houston Rockets in the first round. The Rockets had struggled after a February trade that had sent power forward Otis Thorpe to Portland for Clyde Drexler. First, Drexler needed some time to adjust to his new teammates. Then, just as that adjustment was coming into line, Hakeem Olajuwon was sidelined for two weeks with anemia. Later, after Drexler began taking most of his playing time, Houston's Vernon Maxwell grew dissatisfied and left the team before the playoffs began.

Somehow, despite all the late-season turmoil, the Rockets came together during the playoffs. The Jazz had taken a 2-1 lead in the five-game series, but Houston managed to tie it with a key home win. Utah even had a solid lead late in the fourth quarter of Game 5 in Salt Lake City, but the Rockets closed in a swirl and won the series on a critical late shot.

A few weeks later, I interviewed Jerry Sloan at the league's rookie/free agent camp at Moody Bible Institute in Chicago. I offered my condolences on yet another playoff loss. "It's all right," he said, not sounding entirely convincing. "It's just a f---ing ball game."

From their win over Utah, the Rockets moved on to the semifinals to dispatch Barkley and the Suns in similar wrenching fashion. Barkley and Kevin Johnson had both struggled with injuries, but the Suns had taken a 3-1 series lead over Hakeem and the Rockets, only to see Houston take the last three games of the series, including a 95-94 win in Game 7 that left Barkley and his teammates stunned.

Later, Barkley would tell reporters that for once he'd like to be healthy for a Game 7. "A championship is not that important to me," he said. "I keep hearing how important it is to me. If we win it, all right. If we don't, I'll be all right. I'm not gonna kill myself. I've always felt the same. You guys are trying to tell me how I feel. I'm not like the general public. I don't read your all's sh-- and believe it. If we win it, great. If I don't, I'll still be all right. The sun will still come up tomorrow."

Led by Nick Van Exel, the Los Angeles Lakers had upset the Seattle Super Sonics in the first round, then faced the Spurs in the Western semifinals. It proved to be a nice run for Del Harris' first Los Angeles team, but they were outmatched by the Spurs and fell in six games.

With the win, David Robinson's team advanced to the Conference Finals for the first time in club history. Yet just when they seemed strongest, the Spurs fell apart in the face of a strong challenge from Houston.

"Going into the playoffs we had won 62 games," Jack Haley said, "and we had an extreme air of confidence. We went in and crushed Denver in the first round. The LA series was good for us. Then we went up against Houston and we ran into a situation where good teams expect to win, and uh, Hakeem came out and killed us that first game. But we weren't real concerned because we had won so many games. But when we lost the second game at home we had a complete and total chemistry meltdown. Every single guy started pointing fingers at each other and yelling."

Miraculously, the Spurs lashed back to claim two games in Houston after losing two at home. But with the series knotted at two-all, Spurs management decided to suspend Rodman for the critical fifth game for irritating violations of team rules, i.e., removing his shoes while on the bench, being late to practice, etc.

"All the guys were in favor of playing him," Haley maintained. "Management voted to hold him out. Guys wanted him to play. Winning was most important at that time. Who cares about discipline in the playoffs? The season was over. We were trying to win a championship. It was a huge decision, and it ended up costing us.

"I think had it been Bob Hill's decision, Dennis would have played. Bob and Dennis had a pretty good relationship. He was more about winning ball games. That decision was more from management. I think management felt they could win without Dennis."

The Spurs' season and their best hopes for a championship ended with a Game 6 loss in Houston. In the aftermath, it was clear that Rodman would not remain with the club.

"It was extremely evident that it was over," Haley said of Rodman's tenure. "He and Popovich had hit all all-time low. There was no way. When the playoffs ended, he didn't even fly back with the team. He didn't want to speak with management after the last game. He just took off and went to Vegas and said basically, 'To hell with you.' That was the straw. The Houston series broke the camel's back. His only hope to stay in San Antonio last year would have been for us to win — reaching the Finals wouldn't have done it — we had to win the championship."

END GAME

Meanwhile, the Orlando Magic had eliminated the Indiana Pacers in the Eastern Finals, setting up a meeting between Shaq and Company and the Rockets for the league championship. The Magic were talented but young, evidenced by guard Nick Anderson missing critical free throws that helped Houston win Game 1. From that momentum, the Rockets went on to sweep the best-of-seven series in four games.

In one interview session, a reporter referred to Anderson's missing those early shots as "tragic."

"I've been in worse situations than this," Anderson said quickly. "My high school teammate (Ben Wilson), I watched him die. He got shot twice in the stomach, and I saw it. I was right there, no more than 25 feet away... You grow up on the streets of Chicago, you can see anything. Wednesday night (when Anderson missed key free throws in Game 1) was not a tragedy. It's just something that happens. This was just basketball."

Indeed. And misses are just misses. Airballs are just miscalculations, whiffs in the night, common themes in an NBA season.

Unfortunately, the Houston Rockets' surprising second championship resolved little for the league. The real issue facing David Stern and the players was the need for a collective bargaining agreement. Even as the playoffs were coming to a close, the question loomed: Would there be a strike, as in pro baseball?

At first, no one believed that possible. But as the summer dragged on, and the debate over a new contract grew increasingly acrimonious, the prospects of a work stoppage seemed unavoidable. Even Michael Jordan took sides in the labor issue, moving with a group of renegade players and agents to decertify the players union in hopes that the athletes wouldn't get locked into a deal that Jordan and his agent, David Falk, considered bad. For a time it appeared a majority of the players would side with Jordan and the renegade group, leaving the 1995-96 season in real doubt. But the players union was preserved in a special vote, and an eleventh hour agreement brought the opening of training camp in October.

The new collective bargaining agreement would raise the team salary caps over the next few years to just about $32 million. A decade earlier, it had been less than a tenth of that. Now, the prosperity seemed limitless.

Soon, star players would be pulling in as much as $25 million per season, very strange math for something, to quote Jerry Sloan, that's "just a f---ing game."

SKYWRITING AT NIGHT

CHICAGO, NOVEMBER 1995

It was way back in the '70s when comedian Jimmie Walker quipped that "putting tattoos on a black man is like skywriting at night." Even then he must have had a premonition about Dennis Rodman.

This, of course, is the '90s, and tattoos have become quite popular. Perhaps no one is a greater proponent of body decoration than Rodman, who has a cornucopia of new age symbols etched into his well-muscled arms, shoulders and back. His very first tattoo was scripted on his ankle, the name of model Annie Bakes, who briefly became his wife. Next, inside his left forearm, he had the infant face of Alexis, his daughter, who looks an awful lot like the Gerber baby. ("The Gerber baby?!?" he says when I mention that.) From there, his body has become something of a canvas, or perhaps a punching board, if you count his numerous piercings. To impress another girlfriend he even had his scrotum stapled, but he had to remove the metal because of an infection. Asked what tattoo he plans next, Rodman says, "I don't know. It's gonna be something really tribal on my back." Hearing this makes you think that if anyone seems suited for skywriting at night, perhaps it's Dennis Rodman.

In the wake of the Spurs' loss in the 1995 playoffs, the team's fans spent the summer trying to read the darkened horizon. It seemed certain that Rodman would leave the club. But where would he wind up?

For Rodman, though, there were more immediate items pressing on his agenda. He had to face a civil trial in connection with an Atlanta Hawks dancer's lawsuit allegations that he had given her herpes with unprotected sex. Essentially, Rodman's defense made no attempt to refute that he might have transmitted the condition to her. Instead, Rodman's counsel merely pointed out that the plaintiff was a big girl who should have known to take precaution when having fun, particularly with a technoerotic-pagan like Rodman. That was enough to conclude the case in Rodman's favor with no payoff.

The matter settled, Dennis sought his usual refuge, the craps tables at Vegas, which he visited many times over the summer of 1995, and the arms of Madonna, where the stay was a brief fling at the Hotel Nikko in LA, which provided the setting for yet another media spoof.

"They're having an affair there for a couple of days," Jack Haley explains. "The paparazzi are all over it. There are 20 or 30 of them outside the hotel. Dennis and I are going to Las Vegas. I go to pick Dennis up at the hotel, and I go in through the back door. So I'm upstairs in the room with them, and Dennis and I come down to go to Las Vegas, and I'm carrying my two-month-old infant son. I've got some bags and stuff, so I hand him to Dennis. When Dennis comes out, all the papparazzi go into a feeding frenzy because they think this is Dennis' and Madonna's secret baby. They follow us to the airport snapping photos. It's on 'Current Affair' and 'Hard Copy' and 'E!' saying, 'Here's Madonna's baby.' Of course, when they interview Dennis, they say, 'Is that Madonna's baby? Is that your baby?' Of course, Dennis, being the media hound that he is, says, 'I can't comment on it.' Which is leading them on. Everybody in the country was amused by it, except my wife. She wasn't happy to see her baby being portrayed as Dennis' baby."

For Stacy Haley, the incident was the topper in a long line of irritations. "My wife is not a Dennis Rodman fan by any means," Haley says. "She understands the world that I live in with Dennis. I mean we're very fast-paced. It's a jet-set type of world, and for a married guy, that's not good. But, you know, I'm a tremendous husband and a loving father, and I love my family to death. She knows that, and she also knows that Dennis and I are best friends, and we're going to do our thing. We have a great rapport. . . But my wife does not want a whole lot to do with Dennis and anything we do together. She's not a real big supporter. I mean we're friends, and he comes to our home for holiday dinners and the whole thing. In that type of environment, they're great. But if Dennis and I are going out for dinner and go run around the town at night, that's not good. If we're in Las Vegas together. . . That's not real good."

Of the 19 trips that Rodman and Haley made to Vegas over the summer of 1995, Stacy Haley made one. She, of course, was a mother with two young sons, and while Rodman epitomized several things, family values wasn't one of them. Mainly, he was a creature living on the edge, simply because that's where he knew he could bask in the bright light of celebrity.

"He spent time with Madonna, and when he was with Madonna that increased his time in the public eye and made him more of a star," Haley said of his friend. "Also, he looks at Madonna, the sex book she did and her naked stuff, so now all of the things he does are nude because of the shock value. He talks about, 'Oh, yeah, I hang in the gay community, and I hang out with gay people in gay bars.' That's all shock value. We're best friends; we're together every single night. In the two years I've known him, we've been to one gay bar. But he talks about it all the time, because it's part of his aura and his stigma."

It certainly helped him get a gig with Playboy, a naked photo shoot with a new girlfriend, Stacy, complete with an accompanying story in which he suggested that he would like to do a talk show in drag, The Denise Rodman Show.

The last time he opened up for the magazines, (the cross-dressed *Sports Illustrated* cover), some San Antonio gay basher slashed the tires on his pink truck and wrote FAG on the windshield. Now, however, Rodman had abandoned south Texas to spend the offseason in LA dabbling in show business as Haley hustled to help him find parts. He did a guest spot with Robin Givens on the CBS series "Courthouse," followed by an appearance on Fox's "Misery Loves Company" and a role in Whoopi Goldberg's film, *Eddie*. There was even time to do two 60-second spots for the ASA Psychic Network. All of this was aimed at warming up the film industry for the idea of casting the Worm in a major role.

"We have actually sat down and met with the people from Warner Brothers and Tri Star," Haley said of the film studios. "John Feltheimer, the president of Tri Star, is a very good friend of mine. He's interested in Dennis. What they look for in Dennis is almost a Wesley Snipes type villain, but what Dennis wants is a villain who turns out to be the hero in the end type of thing. I think he would like to do more of a Bruce Willis/*Die Hard* type of role, that type of thing. He's obviously gonna need heavyhitting co-stars to carry him, but I think Dennis will appear in at least one movie. We're very conscious not to put Dennis in any type of basketball movie. We don't want Dennis in a movie where he portrays a basketball player. We want him to break away from that image and play an acting role. We know he can't carry a film. But let's say just for the sake of argument, a Tom Cruise and a Dennis Rodman. Dennis could be second or third billing, but we definitely want major billing. We want him in a film with no other athletes."

There was one little problem. To some degree, Hollywood studio magnates were like NBA general managers. They wanted to know if Rodman would show up. Could he be depended upon? Or would he flake out and hold up expensive production schedules? His desire to be an entertainer and his limited work in television and advertising suggested that he had promise and could be dependable. He had been comfortable and camera-friendly in his Pizza Hut commercial with David Robinson. Yet Rodman's readings and tryouts indicated that he would have to work in a loosely scripted production.

"When Dennis is in an acting situation, and he has to read the script, he looks like an athlete acting," Haley admitted. "But what we've done now with Dennis is said, 'Okay, here's the concept of how we want the dialogue to go. Freelance with it and just talk.' Then he does much better. If he has to say word for word, then he's in trouble."

Within those looser confines, Rodman showed promise. There was little doubt, however, that at least for the time being, his best hopes as an "entertainer" lay with basketball.

As carefree as their privates lives seemed, Haley and Rodman faced some serious questions about their professional futures. Always a fringe player at best, Haley's prospects depended largely on Rodman, and Rodman's prospects, well, they were desperate. First of all, he was nearly broke despite a contract that paid him about $2.5 million annually. He owed substantial amounts of money to both teams he had played for, the Pistons and Spurs, and he hadn't paid his agent in nearly three years. Settling up those accounts after pursuing his rock'n'roll lifestyle for years meant that he had very little left heading into the 1995-96 season. These financial straits meant yet another shift in Haley's role. From teammate to friend to partner in crime, he was now moving toward being Rodman's quasi agent and money manager. Haley set something of a budget for Rodman and made sure that if he was going to Vegas to gamble he kept his bets in a reasonable range. And Haley tried to work it so that Rodman only could go to Vegas if he had earned some extra money from doing a card show or paid autograph session or promotional appearance.

Rodman's contract with the Spurs held only one more season of guaranteed money. But Rodman indicated that he wanted the Spurs to give him $15 million to play another season there. He had no options for imposing that demand other than some type of work disruption, and Spurs definitely wanted no disruptions. "He wanted to stay in San

Antonio," Haley said. "He wanted to play there, but he only wanted to play there if they stepped up to the table and gave him the kind of contract and respect he felt he deserved. They had no intention of doing that."

He had turned 34 on May 13, 1995, an age when most hoop stars are looking at limited futures. It was clear that the Spurs wanted to trade him, rather than deal with another year of headaches. But they were having trouble finding takers. Rodman's ideal scenario was to get with another team for the last year of his contract, perform well and sign a new two- or three-year deal in the neighborhood of $15 million.

"I'll put $5 million in the bank, live off the interest and party my ass off," Rodman told Playboy, just the kind of talk that made NBA general managers very nervous.

Yet, in spite of the harsh criticism directed his way after San Antonio's playoff demise, Rodman still numbered several NBA regulars among his supporters. For example, John Salley of the Toronto Raptors, who was a teammate of Rodman's when the Detroit Pistons won back-to-back NBA championships in 1989 and '90, pointed out to reporters that Rodman was one of the few "real people" in the NBA. And former Boston Celtic guard and Hall of Famer K.C. Jones remarked that in some ways Rodman reminded him of Boston's great center Bill Russell, the wiry 6-9 rebounder, shotblocker and defender extraordinaire who led the Celtics to 11 NBA titles in the 1950s and '60s. Quickness to the ball, selfless defensive mentality and an eccentric streak were characteristics that the two men share, Jones said.

Rodman's history of antics would have been enough to trash the careers and promotional prospects of most athletes. But somehow he was different. Why? Perhaps, in part, because the public apparently responded to his honesty and his sense of humor. Mostly, though, the fans seemed to appreciate the fact that every time he played, he laid his heart on the line. The NBA is populated with pretenders, and as Salley says, Rodman is the "real thing." Whatever that thing might be wasn't exactly clear, but Rodman was correct about one point. He certainly made the NBA more entertaining.

THE STRANGEST BULL

Because of NBA labor troubles, the summer of 1995 required a moratorium on all trades and contract moves, which meant that Rodman's status with San Antonio wasn't resolved until days before training camps were set to open. When a move was finally made, Rodman found sanctuary in the least expected of places, in Chicago, probably the city in the NBA where Rodman was hated most because of his brash intimidation of the Bulls during his days as a Detroit Piston.

"The Pistons called themselves the Bad Boys, and they marketed themselves under that name," Bulls chairman Jerry Reinsdorf had said during a summer interview. "I thought they were thugs, and you know, you have to hold the ownership responsible for that. I mean, Bill Laimbeer was a thug. He would hit people from behind in the head during dead balls. He took cheap shots all the time. Rick Mahorn and Rodman, I mean, they tried to hurt people. It was terrible."

Apparently, however, it wasn't quite terrible enough to stop Reinsdorf, Bulls General Manger Jerry Krause and coach Phil Jackson from acquiring Rodman in a trade with San Antonio last fall. Why? Because the Bulls were desperate for a quality power forward, and Rodman's defense, rebounding and intimidation were just the elements Chicago needed to contend for a fourth league title in 1996. Which prompted the Bulls to begin studying the idea of trading backup center Will Perdue for Rodman.

Phil Jackson, who had always blamed Chuck Daly for the Pistons' rough play, went so far as to ask the former Detroit coach if Rodman would contribute to the team in Chicago and put aside the disruptive behavior that troubled the Spurs over the past two seasons. Daly replied that Rodman would come to play and play hard, which led the Bulls to make the deal after making sure that Michael Jordan and Scottie Pippen weren't opposed to playing with Rodman, whom they both loathed just a few seasons ago.

Jordan and Pippen thought about it, then told Krause to go for the deal. That news elated Rodman, who badly wanted to find a basketball home. "I had no choice," he said. "I feel like I had a lot of negative energy going on in my life, and that was the best way to get rid of it."

Before the trade was consummated, Jackson held extensive talks with Rodman. The discussions convinced Jackson that the eccentric forward could be incorporated into the team. Jackson, who was himself a bit of a rebel as a member of the New York Knicks back in the '70s, grew confident that he could coach Rodman. So the move was made, and as extra insurance for communicating with Rodman, the Bulls signed Haley to a $250,000 contract. Haley would be placed on injured reserve and kept there all season, which allowed him to travel with the team and keep things running smoothly for his buddy.

But just days into training camp, Bulls insiders began to have doubts that the trade was going to work. It seemed Rodman still hadn't spoken to any of his Chicago teammates, and his silence was getting stranger with each passing day.

"It was a tough training camp because everybody was guarded," Haley offered. "Again, you're Michael Jordan. You're Scottie Pippen. Why would you have to go over to Dennis? Michael Jordan made $50 million last year. Why would he have to go over and basically kiss up to some guy to get him to talk? They came over and shook his hand and welcomed him to the team, and this and that. But other than that, it was a slow process."

Rodman's answer to these modest overtures was the basic silent treatment that had driven David Robinson to distraction in San Antonio. Before the Bulls traded for him, Rodman had allowed Jackson to talk to a psychiatrist that Rodman had been seeing recently. The coach came away from the meeting with the shrink thinking that the deal would work, but within days the team's staff members were wondering if there wasn't something the doc had forgotten to mention. Like maybe the fact that Rodman was a raving idiot.

Sports Illustrated came into town the first week of the preseason and wanted to pose one of Bulls star players with Rodman for a cover shot. Jordan, who had a running feud with *SI*, refused to pose. Apparently this time, Rodman wasn't going to wear his dog collar and bustier, but Pippen also declined, saying privately that he didn't want to make a fool of himself.

Finally, the magazine got coach Jackson to do the shot.

It was just one of a string of media squalls stirred up by Rodman's becoming a Bull. In fact, several gay magazines approached the team about securing an interview with Dennis because of his so-called sexual fantasies. Rodman, however, seemed intent on reestablishing his heterosexuality with a guest appearance on the Howard Stern radio show during which he tried to hit up on Stern's female cohost, Robin Quiver.

"Have you ever played on a team where one of your teammates lives with his male hair dresser?" one Chicago reporter asked Michael Jordan during the preseason.

Jordan said he couldn't think of any.

Yet the debate about Rodman's sexuality wasn't the reason his presence seemed a threat to team chemistry. More central to the uneasiness was the relationship between Rodman and Pippen, who had had several well publicized run-ins when the Bulls and Pistons competed in the Eastern Conference Finals in 1988, '89, and '90.

"No, I have not had a conversation with Dennis," Pippen acknowledged early in the year. "I've never had a conversation with Dennis in my life, so I don't think it's anything new now."

Fortunately, things seemed to take a sudden turn for the better with the Bulls' first two exhibition games. First, Rodman's play was stellar. Second, he rushed to Pippen's aid when Indiana's Reggie Miller made some threatening moves. In both games, the crowd obviously adored Rodman, who had come to town with his hair dyed red with a black Bulls' logo in the crown.

"People love to hate Dennis Rodman," Rodman said, as usual addressing himself in the third person. "But once he's on their team, they love Dennis Rodman."

"The very first preseason game of the year," Haley said, "Dennis goes in the game, Dennis throws the ball up in the stands and gets a delay-of-game foul and yells at the official, gets a technical foul. The first thing I do is I look down the bench at Phil Jackson to watch his reaction. Phil Jackson chuckles, leans over to Jimmy Cleamons, our assistant coach, and says, 'God, he reminds me of me.' Whereas last year, any tirade Dennis threw, it was 'Get him out of the game! Sit his ass down! Teach him a lesson! We can't stand for that here!' Here in Chicago, it's more, 'Get it out of your system. Let's go win a game.'"

Rodman also found that rather than fine him $500 for being late to practices, as the Spurs had, the Bulls handled the matter with a light hand. Fines were only five bucks. "Here, first couple of days, he walked in one or two minutes late," Haley said. "Nobody said anything. So now that it's not a big deal, he's on time."

Asked about Phil Jackson early in the year, Rodman replied, "Well, he's laid back. He's a Deadhead, and if he wanted to smoke a joint or two, he would." Rodman laughed hard at this assessment, and when a reporter asked. "Is he your kind of coach?" he replied, "Oh yeah. He's fancy free, don't give a damn. With him it's just, 'Go out there and do the job, and let's go home and have a cold one.'"

Jackson's approach with Rodman soon worked to ease any tensions on the roster. "With Jordan and Pippen, you're talking about two superstars who were not at all threatened by Dennis," Haley said. "They didn't care about his hair color. They don't care about anything. If the man gets 20 rebounds a game and we win, that's all they care about. What he does off the floor, they couldn't care less about that or anything else, as long as he comes to work. And that's what Dennis is about. 'Leave me alone. Let me have my outside life. Let me come do my job as a player. Let my actions on the floor speak for me.' The Bulls have been tremendous for Dennis. Again, everyone just gave him his space, and he just kind of slowly opened up."

Beyond that, Jackson found that Rodman simply "brings a lot of levity to the game." With his raving style, diving for rebounds, challenging opponents, piping off outbursts of emotion, Rodman created one funny circumstance after another. So Jackson sat back and laughed and enjoyed the entertainment. As he had everywhere else he played, Rodman became a crowd favorite in Chicago, where the fans had once absolutely hated him.

"I think they like me," Rodman said when asked about the fans in the United Center. "People gotta realize this business here is very powerful. They can love you or they can hate you, but . . . Chicago fans they hated my guts, and now all of a sudden, I'm like the biggest thing since Michael Jordan. People like me. They like my style, because I'm out there fancy free, you know, doing what I got to do. . . The older I'm getting, the more relaxed I am. I'm just able to say, 'F--- it!' Just say, 'F--- it!'"

One of those pleasantly surprised by Rodman was Tex Winter. The 73-year-old coach found him to have a bright mind for the game. Few players had caught on to the triple-post offense faster than Rodman, although sometimes he didn't like it because it took him away from the basket where he liked to hang to get rebounds. But Winter discovered that Rodman was a hard worker who welcomed coaching. Not only did he accept a coach's opinion, but Rodman sought out Winter to get his thinking on basketball matters. From all appearances, Dennis was going to fit in well.

Yet no sooner had Rodman started to settle in than a muscle injury sidelined him for a month. Even with him on injured reserve, the Bulls rushed out to a 16-2 start, the best in their 30-year history. Then, just as they were expecting his return in early December, news broke about his *Playboy* spread. In the article accompanying the pictorial, Rodman indicated that perhaps Jordan and the league's other stars had been seduced by "the Pedestal," the money and fame of pro basketball. "I bring too much excitement to the game," he said. "Michael Jordan used to do that, but, f--- it, now it's the Dennis Rodman show on the road."

On another team, such outrageousness could have proved devastating. The Bulls, however, shrugged it off as just another blip on their very busy media screen and kept on winning. Rodman's response was to return the second week of December with a monstrous 61 rebounds in just three games. From there, the Bulls bounded on a protracted winning streak, which was accompanied by media reports marveling at Rodman's contribution to the team, at Jackson's deft coaching touch, at Jordan's renewed powers as a superstar. With each victory, speculation mounted as to whether Chicago could win 70 games, breaking the all-time record for wins in a season, set by the 1972 Los Angeles Lakers with a 69-13 finish.

Jerry West, the Lakers vice president for basketball operations who was a star guard on that '72 Los Angeles club, pegged the Bulls as dead ringers to win at least 70 games — unless injuries set them back.

During their big start, the Bulls had toyed with opponents through the first two or three quarters before flexing their power and finishing strong. "We get in that mindset where we can just go out there and beat any team," Rodman explains. "Once we see a team is really being aggressive, all of a sudden we kick in that second gear."

Observers pointed out that with expansion, the NBA is now up to 29 teams, which has thinned the talent base, making it easier for the Bulls to win. Those same observers had conveniently forgotten that in 1972, when the Lakers won, the American Basketball Association was in operation, meaning there were exactly 28 teams fielded in pro hoops between the two leagues.

Whatever the reasons for their success, the Bulls kept churning out victories through the winter of 1996. The sense of power was incredible, greater even than when Chicago won three straight championships, Scottie Pippen said. "Nobody figured that an NBA team could have this type of pace that we're on right now. It's been a lot of fun really, almost like a college atmosphere."

"I think a lot of teams are very afraid of the Chicago Bulls," Rodman said, "just because of who the individuals are, just because they have to concentrate on so many people. A lot of teams are really skeptical. They're saying, 'What are we gonna do now? How are we going to play this team?' They're too worried about how they're going to do that instead of playing us, instead of just going out and playing basketball."

The Bulls presented so many match-up problems that they seemed to mesmerize the opposition. There was Jordan, leading the league in scoring, and Rodman, leading the league in rebounding, and Pippen, leading the league in MVP votes. For help, they had a 6-11 point guard/post-up forward in Toni Kukoc coming off the bench; they had a three-point terror in reserve guard Steve Kerr; a huge body and a talented post passer in Luc Longley; a surprisingly rejuvenated all-purpose guard in Ron Harper; and two backup centers who could score in Bill Wennington and James Edwards.

They also had a mystic for a coach who espoused Native American philosophy and Zen teachings. He talked of the great white buffalo and kept the Bulls headed in the right direction by threatening to make them lose games. In 1992, the Bulls were visiting a similar terror on the league, but Jackson deliberately rested his starters to make sure the team wouldn't win 70. That way, he believed, he set the team up to win the title. Each season presents a mystery, which is why he loves coaching, Jackson explains. "The mystery of this is how well a ball club plays over the course of a season. You know, you make this record run or whatever you're trying to do to try to establish a homecourt advantage. And you get enamored with just winning games, and winning games. But then there's another level that comes at the end of the season. Playoff basketball totally changes everything. That's the mystery, as to whether we can play at this level all through the season and then come through with a championship drive."

In other words, he was worried that his team would get so drunk with winning during the regular season that they wouldn't play sharp ball in the playoffs. Or something like that. If necessary, Jackson planned to slow them down to avoid that.

"You can actually take them out of their rhythm by resting guys in a different rotation off the bench," he explained. "I have considered that."

Such talk only seemed to drive the Bulls harder to keep winning.

"What amazes me most about our team," said Haley, "is that we probably have the league's greatest player ever in Michael Jordan, we have the league's greatest rebounder in Dennis Rodman, and we have what is probably this year's MVP in Scottie Pippen, and what amazes me most is the work ethic and leadership that these three guys bring to the floor night in and night out. With all of the accolades, with all of the money, with all of the championships, everything that they have, what motivates them besides winning another championship? How many months away is that? And these guys are focused now."

Former Bulls assistant Johnny Bach said one of Jackson's special gifts is the ability to establish a clear team structure. "We have in the league a lot of people who think they're a lot better than they are," Bach said. "And that's what coaches have to deal with. Can you get five people to play a team game when all the rewards seem to be for individual achievement? You're talking about fragile egos. Big egos. People who had status and can lose it in this game so quickly. Phil is great at defining roles and having people face up to what the hierarchy is. Here's Michael. Here's Scottie. And he does it in a very intelligent way. He doesn't do it to put you down. But he clearly addresses the problem."

Certainly the professional atmosphere around the Bulls was good for Rodman. It also didn't hurt that he was in the last year of his contract and badly in need of another. The Bulls hoped that as much as anything, would keep him vigilant.

"We're all waiting for the other shoe to drop with Dennis, so to speak," Jackson said in January. "At least the media are kind of looking for that. We're just saying, 'Everything's going good. Just pay attention to basketball and do what comes natural, and that's play and enjoy the game.'"

"The other shoe won't fall because Jack Haley won't allow it to happen," Haley said. "It will not happen. Believe me. Everything is going well. His mind is in the right place. Dennis has finally realized that he's already a superstar. He doesn't need to do this. The other night when he got ejected he took his jersey off and threw it in the stands and had a little one-minute tirade, it was beautiful. It was great. So they fined him $5,000. It's tax deductible.

"It was beautiful. It was part of his thing. If he wants to do that once a month, great. The game was decided. It was over. Hey, no problem. The fans ate it up. They loved that. He can have a tirade as long as it's within the confines of the team."

Haley, though, acknowledged that maybe if anyone was "seduced" by the spotlight, it was Rodman himself. "He has catapulted himself through outrageous hair, tattoos, body piercing and outrageous comments and hardwork basketball, he has catapulted himself to the superstardom of a Magic Johnson or a Michael Jordan," Haley said, "and to someone who's never had that, it's fun, it's exciting. He's one of the biggest names in the game, and he knows exactly why he's there.

"We talked about it the other day. His hair was green, it was fading, it was almost black. I told him, 'Hey, why don't you just let it go black?' He said, 'I can't let it go. My hair is part of my thing. I have to keep it colored. The fans want it. That's what they expect.' So he's very well aware of what has gotten him where he is, and he's very intelligent in what it takes to make himself a star."

Yet Haley knew better than anyone that Rodman's approach, while fun and entertaining, was a high-stakes gamble. "I think the only damaging thing for Dennis is the reluctance for other teams to take a chance on Dennis and to pay Dennis a big contract," he said. "My fear is that he's here; he's playing for his $2.45 million, he's highly underpaid. Yes, Dennis is flying right now, and he's doing everything right. But the question is, at the end of this year does a team, does an owner, does corporate America — basketball is big business — do they want to make that kind of huge investment, $10- to $15- or $20 million, in someone who is unstable? By creating this aura about himself of being unstable and a rebel who's going to fight you at every turn, will that cost Dennis in the long run? That's my greatest fear. That's why we're working so hard this year to turn that around.

"Chicago is a perfect situation for Dennis. He's on a team that's winning. He hates to lose. He's gotta win. He's got a very strong-minded coach who understands him in Phil Jackson. And he has players he looks up to and respects in Scottie Pippen and Michael Jordan. So it's a win-win situation."

"I just go out and do my job and hope it pays off," Rodman said. "I'm having a great time. As long as I do my job, that's the main thing. If I don't do my job, I'm having a bad time."

He loved being in Chicago and loved playing for Jackson. Most of all he loved playing with Jordan and Pippen, who work extremely hard in practice, something that Rodman felt that David Robinson never understood.

"He knows what I like to do, and I know what he likes to do," Rodman said of Jordan. "So I give him the ball every time I can. He wants to go out there and prove to people that a 33-year-old Michael Jordan is not old. He just gets better, just gets craftier, that's all."

This meshing on the court led to a thaw of relationships off it. "What's been really good here is that Michael Jordan and I and Scottie Pippen and I are very good friends," Haley said. "We play a lot of cards together, and we do a lot of stuff off the floor. Dennis has been kind of put in a position, where if we're on the road or something and he wants to go to dinner or he wants to do something with me, and I'm going out with the other guys, then he's kind of forced to come along. He's been put in a situation where, 'Sit in my room and be alone,' or 'Go hang out with my best friend, Jack, who is consequently with Michael and Scottie.'

"Since he has respect for these guys, and since they don't really care, they've gotten through," Haley added. "Michael and Dennis are doing great. Scottie and Dennis still have no conversation really other than basketball. Scottie and Dennis tremendously respect each other, but I don't see those going to dinner too often. I think that goes back to the Piston days, I really do. They'll always play together and be phenom teammates, but when they walk off the floor and it's time to go hang out... No. But Dennis has warmed to this team. For example, two nights ago Steve Kerr, Judd Buechler, Luc Longley, myself and Toni Kukoc all went out. Dennis again had to come along. Once he got out with the guys, he opened up and picked up the tab. These guys were stunned because here we are, midway through the season, and he's out with the guys having a good time."

In an amazing year, Rodman had managed to swing his life around, from his troubles in San Antonio to his seeming triumph in Chicago. As February neared, he became anxious again about making the All-Star team. All-Star Weekend would be held in San Antionio, making a Rodman appearance there very sweet. Although he was high in the fan voting, he wouldn't have enough votes to earn a starting slot, so he would have to depend on the vote of the Eastern Conference's coaches to be named as a reserve.

"We are looking forward to that," Haley said. "We are hoping and praying he makes the team so he can go back to San Antonio and say, 'Hey, look at me now.'"

The coaches, however, overlooked Rodman for the fourth straight year, despite the fact that he was clearly on his way to winning a fifth straight league rebounding title. On his Chicago radio show, Rodman angrily lashed out that the coaches had engaged in a "conspiracy" to keep him out of the game. While conspiracy was a strong word, it was obvious that the coaches at least thought that Rodman had been too disruptive over the past three seasons to reward with All-Star recognition. Depressed, he went to Vegas and rolled bones while the rest of the NBA's elite players went to San Antonio and basked in the kind of limelight that Rodman loved.

Yet if the coaches weren't willing to recognize him, others were beginning to acknowledge his "entertainment value." Earlier in the season, he had finalized a deal with Nike for a new shoe, "Air Worm," which would have frantic styling and unorthodox lacing. "It's wild, man," Rodman said enthusiastically.

Also, Delacourte planned to release a book of his observations titled *As Bad As I Want to Be*.

The real point, however, was that he had made these breakthroughs by being good. "For the first time in his career, through conformity oddly enough, by playing within the lines and showing people he can be a professional," Haley said, "he's now getting business deals."

The Bulls, meanwhile, just kept chugging along at their record-setting pace. They dropped two games just before the All-Star break and stood 46-5 in mid February, but immediately afterward they ran off a 4-0 record, including a key road win at Indiana, to show just how strong their drive was. During the All-Star festivities, Jackson said much of their success would be determined by how their Eastern Conference opponents adjusted to them over the second half of the season. Taking his evaluation as a challenge, the players proceeded to run their record to 57-7, the best effort in the history of an American professional sports team.

Yet even as they succeeded, the skeptics remained cautious, pointing to several potential disasters waiting in the wings. First, Jackson was in the last year of his contract and had done some behind-the-scenes sparring with General Manager Jerry Krause. In March, team chairman Jerry Reinsdorf said that contractual differences had been settled, but Jackson was clearly enjoying his time as a free agent, coaching the most successful team in history.

Secondly, Bach, the Bulls' former defensive coach, worried that Chicago showed an absence of passion in playing defense. The Bulls were still quite effective, Bach said. "But I don't see that identity right now. But I do see with Rodman a superb rebounder on both boards. I see them playing the passing lanes well. They're still a very good defensive team. It applies a blanket to the opponent's best player."

There was also the prospect of injuries, and sure enough, in mid March, Pippen was sidelined with nagging back pain.

The biggest question mark, however, remained Rodman. Would the other shoe fall?

"We're just cruising through right now," he had said earlier in the season. "But we got to keep focused, keep on the right track. If we don't, we'll definitely be out in the first round of the playoffs. Easily."

That, of course, was just the attitude the Bulls had hoped he would show. But on March 16 he was thrown out of a game at New Jersey and responded by head-butting official Ted Bernhardt and throwing a tirade before leaving the court (for which the league fined him $20,000 and suspended him six games, costing nearly another $200,000 in lost salary). Sitting courtside, Jackson laughed. But the incident left the Bulls edged with worry. Were Dennis' demons about to appear? Would he be able to hold the chaos to a minimum the rest of the season so that Jordan and company could claim a fourth title?

The answer, as they all knew, was written in smoke somewhere out there on the multihued skyline of the chilled Chicago night.

EPILOGUE
FORGET PARIS

SPRING 1996

In February 1996, 36-year-old point guard Magic Johnson returned to the Las Angeles Lakers after a four-year hiatus brought on by his HIV-positive status. His effervescent presence helped launch the team on a winning binge that pushed the Lakers right back into serious playoff contention in the Western Conference.

However, the big story of the season remained the Chicago Bulls, who had already won their 60th game by the time spring began to settle on the NBA in March. Although Dennis Rodman had been suspended and Scottie Pippen sidelined by injury, the Bulls had continued winning, pushing their record to a gaudy 70-9 by the final week of the season. It was one of the greatest team accomplishments in the history of modern sport, and it confirmed that Michael Jordan had regained his status as the game's dynamic, dominant player. Night after night he turned in overpowering performances that made Jordan seem, in the words of New York Knicks radio analyst Walt Frazier, "like a man among boys." One night after a game in Charlotte Coliseum, Hornets assistant coach Johnny Bach returned to the empty arena to meet a trio of well-wishers. While talking with them, he retrieved three diamond-laden championship rings from his jacket pocket and held them out for his friends to see. The rings, earned during Bach's days as a Bulls assistant coach, glistened in the arena light.

"I brought 'em in because Matt Geiger (Charlotte's center) asked me," Bach explained. "He wanted to see the championship rings."

Players around the league knew that in all likelihood a look was as close as they would get to a championship this year because Jordan's performances had sent them a grim message: The time of opportunity had passed.

For a young player like Grant Hill in Detroit, this wasn't a particularly difficult fact to accept. With Doug Collins hired as the Pistons coach and Hill coming into his own as a superstar, the future was very bright for Detroit.

But for the aging superstars on other teams, Jordan's presence was a knell in their swan songs.

In seemed that every writer in every NBA city was looking for signs of aging in Utah's John Stockton and Karl Malone. But nobody looked harder for those signs than Utah coach Jerry Sloan. Each time after a difficult loss, Sloan would get up the next day and look in his players' eyes for signs that they were finally getting weary of competing. Each time, he was relieved to find the fire still smoldering that had driven Stockton and Malone to miss only eight games between them in a combined 23 seasons.

Sloan knew his team lacked the talent of most other upper-echelon NBA clubs, yet each year the Jazz shoved their way near the top simply because of the competitiveness of his two stars. Sloan badly wanted to win a title, but his real mania was the effort, the intensity. He wanted no part of a team just going through the motions.

"As long as we compete, I can live with that," Sloan said quietly.

In Phoenix, Charles Barkley was deciding what he, too, could live with. It had been a long difficult season for Barkley and his Suns teammates. A run of injuries had left them struggling to remain in the playoff pack and had brought the firing of coach Paul Westphal, a Barkley favorite.

A championship is not that important to me," Barkley said. "I keep hearing how important it is to me. If we win it, all right. If we don't, I'll be all right. I'm not gonna kill myself...The sun will still come up tomorrow."

To help digest this implied resignation, Barkley seemed to rely more than ever on his sense of humor. A perfect example of this was his off-handedness at the All-Star Weekend in San Antonio, when he held court for a group of reporters in the locker room about 90 minutes before game time.

He was expressing his views on a variety of subjects when a member on the NBA's international public relations staff appeared and asked Barkley to give an interview to a French magazine writer named Olivia.

"Pleased to meet you," Barkley said. "You got some beautiful eyes, Olivia."

She blushed and stammered, "Thank you very much."

EPILOGUE

"Where are you from?" he asked.

"Paris," she said and asked if he was nervous about playing.

"No," he said. "I'm great at what I do, and I get fun out of playing."

"Is it difficult to have a private life?" she asked.

"It's very difficult. I have no private life."

"No?"

"These other people have no lives," he said, nodding at the reporters standing around him. "so they have to worry about my f---ing business. That's the American way."

"And you're not nervous for the match?" she asked again, referring to the upcoming game.

"Oh, honey," he said, "if you're gonna be coming over here, you can't be calling my game no 'match.'

"Tell my girl if she's gonna be covering me, she can't be calling my game a 'match,'" he said to the NBA public relations staffer. "You got to work on your girl."

Olivia was obviously nonplussed by this minor gaffe, but like a good journalist, she quickly resumed her questioning.

"So do you have any private life?" she asked.

"No private life."

"Any girlfriends?"

"Several," Barkley said and chuckled, sending the room into loud laughter.

"Several?" Her eyes grew wide. "They're lucky."

"They're lucky?" Charles asked, eyeing her.

"Yes," she said with the slightest gulp.

"No," he confessed. "I have a wife."

"A wife? And some children?"

"One," he said, "that I know of." Again the reporters laughed.

"How old is it?" Olivia asked.

"She's six," he said.

As Barkley replied, another NBA representative came into the locker room and asked him to go to another room for a photo shoot.

"Do you know what you're going to do after basketball?" Olivia asked.

"Nothing, hopefully," he said. "I haven't decided yet what I want to do."

Barkley then turned to the assembled players and media in the room and announced, "Everybody, this is Olivia from Paris. How is Paris?"

"Oh," she said, "you don't know Paris?"

"I've been there one time," Barkley said. "I was drunk. I don't remember much. It was good while I was there. I wasn't there long."

"Did you see the Eiffel Tower?" she asked.

"The Eiffel Tower?" he raised his eyebrows. "No. You know, I think I saw it one day. It was kind of blurry. No, Paris is nice. I had a good time over there. A lot of rich people."

"Yeah, some poor people, too," she said.

"Poor people? I try not to hang out with them unless I have to," Barkley said with a quick wink.

Olivia asked to see Barkley's shoes.

"Not only can you see them, you can buy some," he said. "They sell 'em. For like 140 bucks."

"Thank you," she said.

"You're welcome. Nice to meet you," he said before heading off to the photo shoot.

In the hallway outside the locker room he encountered a little old lady who wanted him to pose with her for a snapshot. Immediately accommodating, Barkley draped his arm around her and smiled for the camera.

Coming around a corner was Rod Thorn, the league's vice president for enforcement, who saw Barkley with the little old lady and exclaimed, "Oh my god, the beauty and the beast!"

How true that was. Sir Charles, standing there with his freshly shaved head glistening, was a beauty and a beast, all wrapped in one 252-pound package.

The next instant, Barkley turned and was headed off to the photo shoot, his laughter ringing in the hallway, an echo perhaps of what might have been.

Bibliography

Extensive use was made of a variety of publications, including the *Baltimore Sun, Basketball Times, Boston Globe, Chicago Defender, Chicago Tribune, Chicago Sun-Times, Daily Southtown, The Detroit News, The Detroit Free Press, The Daily Herald, Hoop Magazine, Houston Post, Houston Chronicle, Inside Sports, Los Angeles Times, The National, New York Daily News, The New York Times, New York Post, The Charlotte Observer, USA Today, The Oregonian, Philadelphia Inquirer, San Antonio Express-News, Sport, Sports Illustrated, The Sporting News, Street & Smith's Pro Basketball Yearbook,* and *The Washington Post.*

Also vital were several books, including:
24 Seconds to Shoot by Leonard Koppett
Bull Session by Johnny Kerr and Terry Pluto
Cages to Jump Shots by Robert Peterson
Championship NBA by Leonard Koppett
From Muscular Christianity to the Market Place by Albert Gammon Applin II
From Set Shot to Slam Dunk by Charles Salzberg
Giant Steps by Kareem Abdul-Jabbar and Peter Knobler
Holzman on Hoops by Red Holzman and Harvey Frommer
Honey by John Russell
Long Time Coming by Chet Walker and Chris Messenger
Loose Balls by Terry Pluto
March to the Top by Art Chansky and Eddie Fogler
Maverick by Phil Jackson and Charlie Rosen
Michael Jordan by Mitchell Krugel
Official Spalding Basketball Guide, various editions, 1898-1930
Pro Basketball Encyclopedia by David S. Neft and Richard M. Cohen
Rare Air by Michael Jordan with Mark Vancil
Sportswit by Lee Green
Tall Tales by Terry Pluto
The Bob Verdi Collection by Bob Verdi
The Bulls and Chicago by Bob Logan
The Franchise by Cameron Stauth
The Glory and the Dream by William Manchester
The History of Professional Basketball by Glenn Dickey
The Jordan Rules by Sam Smith
The Official NBA Basketball Encyclopedia, edited by Zander Hollander and Alex Sachare
Transition Game by Melissa Isaacson

"The best, most in-depth book ever written on the Lakers."
— Kareem Abdul-Jabbar

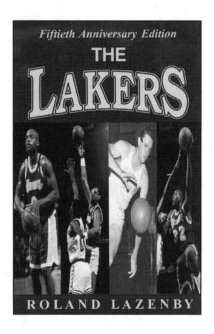

Much more than a dusty recounting of games won and lost, *The Lakers* is charged with the dreams, triumphs and disappointments that have driven the Lakers for five decades. Colorful, immediate, written with a flair and a deep understanding of the game, *The Lakers* is splendid reading for any basketball fan. Ask for it at your local bookstore! ISBN 1-57028-062-2